The Capital That Couldn't Stay Put

The Complete Book of California's Capitols

by

June Oxford

James Stevenson Publisher
1500 Oliver Road Suite K-109
Fairfield, California 94533
(707) 434-0210

Table of Contents

Acknowledgements

The story of California's migrating capital intrigued me long before I wrote *The Capital that Couldn't Stay Put.* The Capitol Restoration provided the impetus and inspiration that led to the finished manuscript.

Writing the book deepened my already high regard for libraries, particularly, Bancroft Library, Berkeley; California State Library, Sacramento; San Jose State University Library, San Jose; West Valley Community College Library, Saratoga; Sunnyvale Public Library; Santa Clara Public Library; and San Jose Public Library.

Many people shared information and provided encouragement. An interview with Senator James R. Mills was helpful in understanding aspects of the restoration. I owe thanks to persons who worked on the Capitol Restoration Project, especially Raymond Girvigian, F.A.I.A., Historical Restoration Consultant, who gave me a copy of his *Restoration and Development of the Capitol for the Joint Committee on Rules California State Legislature*, Volume 2, and to Lucinda Woodward, Interpretive Historian and President of the Sacramento County Historical Society, for her *A Documentary History of California's State Capitol.*

Marvin Brienes, State Park Interpreter with the California Department of Parks and Recreation, conducted an extensive oral history of the Capitol Project. I read some of the interviews that had been typed and edited. Brienes also gave me useful information in an interview and suggested resources.

Courtesies extended by John Kolb, Museum Manager; Wendy Welles Franklin, Head of Collections; and Heidi Casebolt, Assistant Head of Collections, all at the California State Capitol Museum, are very much appreciated. Lynn Marlowe, in charge of the Photo Collection, gave generously of her time and expertise.

Valuable information and insights were gained from interviews with James DeJournett, Associate Landscape Architect; and Michael Casey, dedicated craftsman and recipient of a National Craftsman Award from the American Institute of Architects.

I'm grateful for the support of writer-friends, particularly, Annemarie Berg and Olive Engwicht, who read parts of the manuscript.

My sister, Mary West, assisted in the final proofreading.

My sincere thanks to Leonard McKay, publisher, editor, and photographer, for his many suggestions and excellent advice.

CHAPTER I
Restoration of the Capitol

Because "capital" and "capitol" are pronounced alike, they're apt to be confused. According to Webster, "capital" refers to the city that serves as the location of government. "Capitol" is the building in which the legislature convenes. Sacramento is the capital of California. The legislature meets at the Capitol in Sacramento.

Returning the 108-year-old Capitol to its former grandeur, has been called "the nation's most extensive and complex restoration project."

In essence, the Capitol was a museum filled with artifacts. Dismantling had to be done using the painstaking techniques of an archeological dig, with the same precision: careful measuring, photographing, and cataloging.

Reconstruction presented a series of challenging problems. The complexity and uniqueness of the project made the teamwork of historians, architects, contractors, structural engineers, craftsmen, and the 2000-plus people who worked on the project essential. Restoration started in 1976 and took five-and-one half-years, but the story started long before.

In 1971, the legislature authorized a structural report on the soundness of the Capitol in the event of an earthquake. The report concluded: Even a mild earthquake would cause the building to collapse.

The Rules Committee decided a corroborating opinion would be in order. State Architect, Fred Hummel's 108-page report reached the same conclusion: "In a strong earthquake the trusses over the Senate and Assembly would collapse, dropping the fourth floor into the Legislative Chambers below. The dome and cupola might collapse down into the rotunda."

The lime mortar had disintegrated over the years until the building was supported virtually by "gravity and habit." In addition, scars remained from the 1906 remodeling. Trusses supporting the fourth floor were not attached to the walls. Ducts for plumbing, heating, and air conditioning honeycombed the building.

Signs, "Off Limits To The Public," appeared at the Capitol entrances. Legislators still met in the Assembly and Senate Chambers; supposedly, they understood the risks. The public could observe the legislature from the galleries, only if they signed waivers of any liability.

Legislators were shown color slides of San Francisco's City Hall in ruins after the quake. Some started wearing hard hats to bring the unsafe conditions of the Capitol to the attention of the public.

Most executive offices moved to other buildings in 1973. Ivy Baker Priest, then Treasurer, stayed in the Capitol. She opted to take her chances, rather than risk state funds of $10 billion, mostly in negotiable securities, in a building without proper safeguards.

Added to the crisis was a space crunch, which many thought needed to be solved as much as unsafe conditions.

In the late 1960's, plans for a new Capitol were proposed. The building consisted of two twin 17-story office buildings with legislative chambers nestled between. The offices projected space needs to the year 2000.

The plan became known as Collier Towers, named for its single-minded advocate Senator Randolph Collier. Eventually, he and his allies obtained approval of a $42 million appropriation. Two private consulting firms recommended building "Collier Towers" and abandoning the Capitol. Mock-ups were made of the Towers.

There were others who favored restoration of the Capitol. Legislative leadership changed. Senator James R. Mills, a former history teacher and museum curator, gave his views favoring restoration in a *Sacramento Bee* article. When the governor's liaison contacted Mills and asked how then-Governor Reagan could help, Mills replied, "It would be helpful if the Governor made a public statement." The American Council of Architects, and other civic and cultural groups went on record as supporting the Capitol restoration. The Bicentennial gave impetus to preservation and sparked interest in our historical heritage. Proponents of Capitol restoration won out.

In 1974, $42 million was appropriated to give the Capitol a new lease on life.

The legislators moved into a temporary home, connected to the East Annex, in 1976. The steel-framed, heavy-duty "pre-fab" was built to withstand earthquakes.

Events moved swiftly at first. Governor Jerry Brown signed the bill in August 1975. In September, Welton Becket Associates were hired as architects on the basis of a two volume report, the first analyzing space needs, the second dealing with historic preservation. The next month Continental-Heller/Swinerton & Walberg were signed as contractors. URS/John A. Blume & Associates served as the structural engineers.

Planning began in December. The first step was to set goals. The main concern was simply safety, bringing the building up to modern earthquake standards. Secondly, it was to serve as functional work space for the legislature with provisions for T.V. cameras and electronic voting systems. Also, the Capitol would be restored to its former elegance, and serve as a Museum, where people could step back in time and gain an understanding of the changes in government and its growth. Moreover, the Capitol was to evoke an appreciation of its beauty and a sense of pride in their government of all who entered.

The time period chosen for restoration, basically 1900 to 1910, allowed for such amenities as eleva-

During the restoration, steel beams, called shoring and bracing, supported the exterior walls while the interior strengthening was done.
Photo by Dale Dwyer, California State Capitol Museum Collection

tors, electric lights, telephone systems, improved plumbing. The different dates included the pre-1906 elegant architectural features and the 1906 fourth floor addition.

Every area of the building, every nook and cranny was measured. There were only a few early architectural drawings to help. The original drawings were lost in the 1862 flood. The duplicates were burned in a fire. Eight people spent three months making a complete set of drawings. Numerous structural corings were taken for evaluation, so methods could be devised to make the building structurally sound.

John Worsley, owner's representative and former State Architect explains, "We built and rebuilt the Capitol on paper, until we came up with a sequence which permitted us to save most of the building."

For awhile, lawsuits troubled the Capitol restoration. The Pacific Legal Foundation, an alliance of taxpayer organizations and contractors, protested that state law required competitive bidding.

Photo of the golden poppy tile is on display in the museum. The original tiles are back on the second floor of the Capitol.
Photo by Leonard McKay

The Foundation also argued that the Capitol contract provided minority-owned companies receive 20% of the sub-contracts. Both lawsuits lost, on the basis that the Capitol was a unique, complex project with special requirements. However, the resulting delays were costly.

The Capitol interior had to be stripped before construction work began. Most important of all, records had to be kept with the fussiness of a supercautious accountant, if there were to be no missing artifacts. A computer system was devised to help keep track of the innumerable items.

In no instance could a door, window sill, or molding be ripped out. It had to be removed by hand and marked with the exact location of its removal. It would be refinished, perhaps repaired, and put back in the same spot.

Piece by piece, the paintings, the legislators' desks, the floor tiles were taken to two warehouses.

There was an excitement to the work.

At times, workers found treasures hidden behind former remodelings. Acoustical tile covered a frescoed ceiling. Removing the murals on the rotunda walls revealed niches decorated with hand-painted marbelizing.

Sometimes, they came across signatures of workers that had been there 100 years before—at the top of an intricately carved door or worked into the design of a frieze.

"Each time there was a sense of being linked to the past," said Heidi Casebolt, Assistant Head of Collections. "Of course, we left our names, too. Perhaps, someone a hundred years from now will discover them."

The quest for authenticity was pursued by a 12-person team from the California Department of Parks and Recreation and architect-historian Raymond Girvigian; fervid believers that "integrity of restoration depends on the evidence unearthed." They poured over boxes of long-forgotten, handwritten letters in the State Archives, bills for materials, documents, newspaper articles and scrutinized old photos to verify furnishings for the museum rooms.

Notes were made of small items as well as large, such as the wastebaskets, the flowers, the type of hat hanging on the hatrack.

Flyers went out, alerting people who might have acquired furniture at a state auction of surplus material. A leather chair, now in Governor Pardee's office, was found on a front porch. Originally, fifty-

One of Governor Budd's secretaries. This photo was used in creating part of the museum room of Governor Pardee's Main office.   Sacramento Museum and History Department Collection

five fireplaces had inadequately heated the Capitol. The marble mantels sold for $1.00 each, when they were considered surplus. The mantels on view today are mostly antiques.

Some of the furnishings had been lent to other government offices. Some had gone to state mental hospitals. Heidi Casebolt tells of going to Stockton State Hospital. "The piece I was looking for wasn't there, but the secretary said she would keep an eye open for any record that showed its whereabouts. Sure enough, it had been sent to Columbia State Historic Park. Eventually, it was returned to us."

"First we searched for the original, then a duplicate, and as a last resort a reproduction was made," Casebolt related.

The list lengthened to 10,000 hard-to-find items.

First the team looked locally, then scoured the state. They went East, when the items couldn't be found in California.

Alberta Curley found a rare Renaissance revival table, nicknamed "puppy dog table" after the carved dogs at the ends, at a Massachusetts antique fair for dealers. It seemed to be the exact one in a photograph of the Treasurer's Office, but since it couldn't be documented, they are calling it a duplicate.

Odd things were found as the crew searched for clues to aid in reproducing ceilings, paint schemes, and furnishings. Even though the basement had been

thoroughly cleaned and fumigated in 1899, it still held remnants of long ago.

In at least one instance, the find was horrifying. During the 1906 remodeling workers had poured a continuous loft of concrete, raising the brick wall eighteen inches to support the fourth floor. Later, the extension of the wall was mistaken for a beam and the bricks removed. Only the bond to the slab above remained as support. Workers gutting the interior, found one section that had crashed to the third floor, breaking into pieces weighing 3,000 pounds each. Four more were found in the building.

The historic bronze elevator doors on the first, second and third floors are both originals and reproductions. Workmen pulled off a wall above the elevators to reveal a delicate filagreed transom. The set of transom grills was restored, and together with architect's drawings, used to recreate the balance.

Not a fragment of carpet was found. Researchers perused old photos for patterns and spent time in museum archives. Carpet manufacturers experimented with colors and patterns to be sure of accuracy before the final weaving.

Searchers for original paint colors were helped by a xenon flash lamp, a modern device that removed three or four coats of paint.

A portion of the frieze, reproduced for the Archives Room, was hidden behind a heating duct. Architectural fragments, used as clues to recreate a portion of the coffered ceiling of the assembly, were found under the floor beneath the podium, left by workers during the 1906 remodeling.

Meanwhile, the team of architects, structural engineers, design engineers, and contractors went about devising means of structural strengthening for the building. The weakness of the brick walls was the biggest problem.

Since the Capitol was nearly symmetrical, work was done in three phases. The south wing would be braced and shored first. When that wing was completed, the bracing would be transferred to the north wing. The difficult rotunda was left until last.

Once the shoring was in place, the roof and fourth floor were removed.

The construction methods used seem upside down at first glance. They started from the top and worked down. It had definite advantages. Working from the ground up would have left an unsupported brick wall.

The method that made it possible is called wet process shotcrete. Essentially, it is a concrete mix that can be sprayed under pressure making forms unnecessary. Also, tests proved the original foundation had settled very little. Since the weight of the shotcrete equalled that of the brick that was removed, a new foundation was not required.

A 12-inch layer of brick was peeled back in 60-foot sections. Shotcrete was sprayed on to equal the 30-inch thickness of the old walls. At intervals, the brick was reinforced with steel bars embedded in place with epoxy resin. The old brick and new cement bonded together to form a strong unit.

When the first portion cured, workers could proceed to the next portion. When the procedure reached just above the third floor, that floor was removed. The whole process was repeated to the second floor, all the way down to the basement.

At the basement level, the wall was stopped three-and-one-half-feet above the foundation. A three-foot thick concrete slab basement floor was poured. Needle beams 2' x 3' were inserted into the walls and foundation slab, using a coring machine. They anchored and tied it all together.

Once the foundation cured, new interior walls and floors were built in the conventional manner. Identical methods were used in the north wing.

The rotunda presented problems. The basement floor of the rotunda was removed down to bare dirt. New concrete footings supported pipe columns for the first floor slab. The doughnut-shaped second floor balcony was removed. Then a new second floor could be poured resting on the pipe supported from the first floor.

On these two solid floors, pipe scaffolding could be constructed to support the inner dome. The unreinforced brick of the inner dome (the one viewed looking up from the rotunda) was strengthened with sprayed concrete. Twenty-four 2' x 3' needle beams supplied necessary additional support, transferring the weight of the dome to the rotunda walls.

The difficult part was finished. Now came the part that seemed impossible. The brick piers, supporting the drum for the upper dome, (the one viewed from the outside) were in poor shape. How could they be replaced without taking down the dome?

It was done in small steps. The upper dome wall was first braced with new concrete work and needle beams. Then it was rebuilt and strengthened with concrete pilasters. Next the lower drum was reinforced with poured concrete and needle beams to act as a base for new concrete piers. As the last step, the 24 piers were carefully replaced two at a time.

The dome leaked from the day it was constructed. Oldtimers remember puddles on the rotunda floor after heavy rains. This time the dome would lose its historic leak.

Mock ups were built and analyzed on the warehouse grounds. The final model used overlapping copper shingles attached to a wood backing with cleats, allowing for expansion and contraction. Karl Mindermann, a sheet metal worker for Park Mechanical,

devised a special machine to stamp out 300 copper panels, each with a curled lip to seal out rain. Also, hidden troughs were added. The 24 standing ribs of the dome were removed, countless dents hammered out, and replaced on top of the new copper roof.

Mindermann earned a national craftsmanship award from the American Institute of Architects for his work. He insists his five co-workers deserve equal credit.

What color was the lofty copper dome to be?

The legislators debated over the important matter. In 1948, the dome had been painted an ugly mustard-yellow to celebrate the 100th anniversary of the gold discovery. Some wanted the restored dome to be gold plated; others wanted it given the green patina of age by using uric acid. Finally, it was decided to let the copper age naturally.

Some 1,500 artisans and craftsmen played a vital part on the team. Old-time crafts had to be relearned, ingenious methods devised, and new materials used in the restoration.

Robert Mathews, project director for Welton

The building was gutted on either side of the rotunda and new reinforced concrete was tied to the old brick walls. The grey walls show this new reinforcement.

Photo by Dale Dwyer, California State Capitol Museum Collection

Becket, praises, "We had the best talent in the state on this job and it shows."

The renovated tile floors represent a marvel of workmanship and patience. Hans Scharff, Los Angeles mosaicist, personally supervised the restoration of the marble mosaic tile on the second floor. The floors were photographed with an aerial camera, then cut in four feet sections with a diamond saw and shipped to Los Angeles. The tile design, with golden California poppies in its center and corners, was broken apart, cleaned and repaired. Then Scharff put the 600,000 pieces, each no larger than an inch, back together again on sheets of paper. It was planned so that when it was turned out on the floor the paper would be on top. When it came back to the Capitol, the tile was cemented in place and the paper dissolved with water.

A new version of the old Minton-Maw tile imported from England was laid on the second floor balcony of the rotunda. The original tile floor featured an intricate geometric pattern of small tiles in red, buff, black, brown, and white. The English tile was made from clay powder. The restoration utilized standard unglazed quarry tile to nearly match the original in texture and color. Working from photos, apprentice Kim Stoddard (for Fisher Tile and Marble Inc.) painstakingly cut more than 50,000 pieces for the 2,500 square feet area. Of uneven thickness, the tiles had to be laid carefully with extra mortar applied by hand for a level surface.

Close-up of Minerva on first floor tile.
Photo by Lynn Marlowe, California State Capitol Museum Collection

A new version of the old Minton-Maw tile was laid on the second floor rotunda. The new is a standard quarry tile; original tile is at the stair landing and was from England.
Photo by Dale Dwyer, California State Capitol Museum Collection

Applying plaster mixture to frieze for Parget ceiling in Archive Exhibit Room.

Photo by Dale Dwyer, California State Capitol Museum Collection

The original Minton-Maw tile was renovated and relaid on the stair landing. The tile was chemically treated to remove dirt following instructions from ceramicists who had worked at Hearst Castle. Bob Dunham was pulled off his job of blasting exterior walls to become a craftsman. The entire floor was laid out in the warehouse before it was taken back to the Capitol. "I counted 18,000 pieces," says Dunham. He called the job "three months of slavery."

Tile in the first floor corridor duplicates the original pattern, laid down in 1896. The 6" x 6" tiles depict the Roman goddess of wisdom, Minerva; a grizzly bear; and the word "Eureka." Its theme emulates the state seal. The staff of Heath Ceramics, Sausalito, experimented to get the proper grid effect of the original Minerva mural. Over 500 stainless steel screens were required to produce the different shades and colors of the beautiful, durable corridor floor.

The technique used to create the intricate plaster work of the ceilings and friezes, called parget, was a lost art. Michael Casey experimented, using a commercial joint compound mix squeezed through a pastry tube. "We learned by trying it out, wiping it off if it didn't look right, and trying again."

Casey, Bob Dunham, and sculptor Diane Buettler, formed the team responsible for the pargeted frescoed ceilings in the Museum Rooms and the Senate and Assembly Committee Hearing Rooms. "Sometimes, we only had fragments and had to use creativity," says Casey.

Casey calls it "pastry tubing. It looks delicate, but it took a lot of strength to do." The Archives Room ceiling is a prime example of their work.

"To reach the ceilings in the Archives Room, we used a hydraulic lift, called a scissors lift. An entire floor of scaffolding was built in the Senate and Assembly Committee Hearing Rooms. We tried lying down to work, but found standing up was best, even though we developed cricks in our necks."

After putting in an eight hour day "pastry tubing," Casey went home and worked on a five-foot sculpture of Minerva for the Senate. He also made molds for the rotunda. Of his work, Casey says, "I try to imitate the original craftsman. If I'm doing my job as a restorationist, my hand and style shouldn't show."

Like most of their fellow craftsmen, his team left their signatures—in parget ten inches high—hidden in the Archives Room. Casey received a National

Recreated monumental stairway leading to Senate and Assembly chambers.   *Photo by Leonard McKay*

"Craftsman of the Year" award for his innovative handiwork.

Barbara Basten was pulled from her carpentry job to refinish the walnut railing on the second floor of the rotunda. She took five months to take apart the 300 pieces, scrub, sand with five grades of sand paper, reassemble, and refinish. Except for the base, added to protect peering children from falling, the railing is original.

The monumental stairways leading from the front entrance to the Senate and Assembly were replicated by Burnett & Sons Mill & Lumber Company. A newel post from the original stairs, ripped out in 1906, was discovered in a Sacramento church. The post and old photos, along with a layout block discovered behind a marble facade, served as guides. Since there was no walnut long enough, Honduras mahogany substituted for the original wood.

"In all our hundreds and hundreds of stairs, these were the most ornate," said Burnett Miller, owner. The job was a direct link with the past for Miller. His great, great grandfather, who founded the company

Bear's head on newel post carved by Robert Orr.
Photo by Leonard McKay

Grand stairway.
Photo from the California State Library Collection, circa 1890

The rotunda during restoration.
Photo by Lynn Marlowe, California State Capitol Museum Collection

in 1870 and was also a stairbuilder, worked on the original stairs.

Miller imported wood carvers from Los Angeles and Nevada City to do the extensive carving. Robert Orr, who carved the three bears' heads for each newel post, carved 98 grizzly heads in all for the Capitol restoration.

Some artisans came out of retirement to revive lost arts.

Wood graining enjoyed popularity during the Victorian period. Inexpensive pine and fir were given the look of oak by swirling paint about with little combs and brushes. Redwood, considered "common," was also grained. Practical items, such as safes and water coolers, were wood grained to disguise their humble features. Examples of all of these can be seen in the Capitol Museum.

Repairing the delicate-looking cast iron ornaments at the top of the fluted columns presented a challenge. The wrought iron bolts connecting them to the columns, originally the thickness of a finger in size, had corroded to the width of a fingernail. Some had

already fallen off the building. Weighing from 10 to 70 pounds, each was removed and cataloged. They were sand-blasted, painted white, and re-anchored with stainless steel screws.

The lead paint used on the cast iron ornaments was a health hazard. A safe method of removing the paint was developed and monitored carefully.

A particularly ingenious arrangement solved the problem of concealing electrical equipment and valves that would need frequent repairs. They were hidden above removable rosettes decorating the light fixtures.

There were innumerable problems of repair and reproduction that had to be solved. The massive 15-foot-high doors to the portico were steamed to eliminate warping. The "lincrusta," a linoleum-like wallpaper made to look like embossed leather, was reproduced using cast plaster and fiberglass.

The rotunda is the crowning glory of the restoration. Its subtle colors, its spiraling lines, its soaring dome, both startle and soothe the senses. To walk into the rotunda, is to be immersed in a sea of color—

Applying glue to dome decoration. Next, thin sheets of Dutch metal, a gold-leaf imitation, will be applied.
Photo by Dale Dwyer, California State Capitol Museum Collection

pinks, lavenders, shades of blue, soft yellows, buffs, and golden glitter. The effect, surprisingly, is harmonious rather than garish.

The color scheme was based on analysis of plaster fragments and colors in use during the American Renaissance period. Only black and white photos were available. Frank Bouman with 50 years of experience in decorative painting, and Raymond Girvigian, architect-historian, combined their expertise for the planning.

The imaginative "Flying Griffin" murals on the rotunda walls were based on originals from an old photo and use of xenon flash to remove paint covering the original designs. Frank Bouman painted the murals on canvas panels in Los Angeles, and they were glued on the walls later.

Bouman coaxed his brother, Tom, out of retirement to marbelize the niches in the same rosy-pink hue. The profusion of gold trim is Dutch metal, a gold-leaf imitation, with all the glitter of gold, but one/tenth the cost.

A checkerboard of black and white marble tiles covers the floor.

On the balcony, the railing is the original walnut, refinished and polished. Floors are a geometric pattern of quarry tiles, a look-alike reproduction of the original imported English tile. Sixteen original cast iron bear heads, with bright red tongues, are mounted on medallions around the walls. Everywhere, there's lavish gold highlighting.

In the next tier, the panels are more purple than pink, with blues in beading and rich detailing.

Sixteen garlands border the upper tier. Michael Casey made the molds for these. They were sent to San Francisco to be cast in plaster.

The spiraling lines of the rotunda's four tiers draw the eye to the dome. The upper dome, painted lighter than the rest, intensifies the soaring effect of the 120 foot height.

Actually, you're looking at the inner dome, 90 feet below the cupola of the outer dome. Twelve small windows edged with tiny lights, and the "dome's eye" radiate light to the rotunda.

Robert Mathews, project director for Welton Becket, says, "You never walk into the building without looking at the rotunda. It's an awesome piece of work."

Michael Casey, a five year veteran of the restoration project, pays tribute to the oldtime craftsmen versed in the antiquated techniques of gold leafing, stenciling, marbelizing and decorative painting: "I learned so much just watching them. It was a chance to care about the work I did. I got more out of the building than I put into it."

The perfection of the rotunda is not happenstance. Frank Bouman practiced on a rendering, before he and his three helpers tackled actual rotunda walls.

The restored Senate Chamber echoes the traditional color scheme of the British House of Lords. The red rug is the same design as the Assembly. Walls are pink and shades of red.

The restored original desks, inset with red leather, have been equipped with microphones. The rostrum furniture is also original.

The motto: *Senatoris est Libertatem Tueri*, lettered in gold over the President's desk is a reminder that "A Senator's duty is to guard the liberty of the commonwealth." The restored portrait of George Washington, attributed to Jane Stuart, is crowned with the gold State Seal. A five-foot sculpture of Minerva overlooks proceedings. Electronic gear and television systems are hidden behind shutters and red draperies.

The restoration brought elegance back to the Senate. The six-hundred pound crystal chandeliers were authentically recreated, based on historical photos. Elaborate moldings and pendants ornament the ceiling. The gallery wraps around the sides as it did originally. The gallery seats are originals.

By 1862, the number of Senators in the legislature had grown to 40. The Constitution of 1879 set the Senate at that number. More traditional than the Assembly, the Senate still votes by voice.

The Assembly Chamber echoes the traditional color scheme of the British House of Commons. A mint green rug covers the floor, with walls in softer tones of green.

The original walnut desks, inset with green leather, have been refinished and equipped with microphones and electronic voting buttons. The rostrum furniture is also original.

The goldlettered motto over the Speaker's desk, *Legislatorum est Justas Leges Condere* states, "The duty of the Legislature is to make just laws." Over the rostrum is a 19th century portrait of Abraham Lincoln. A system of sliding panels and shutters conceals the electronic voting, television, and security systems. The historic dais had to be adapted to house a minicomputer and control system. The Assembly makes extensive use of electronic equipment. Concealing the technology so the chamber could present a historic face, called for ingenious devices.

Chandeliers, gallery, and opera-type seats are like those used in the Senate Chamber. The Corinthian columns and gold highlighted pilasters have been returned. Pride of the Assembly is the coffered ceiling with its California wildflower design. Frag-

Chandeliers in Assembly Chamber.
Photo by Lynn Marlowe, California State Capitol Museum Collection

Governor Pardee's Main Office, 1906. This photo was used to create the house museum room.
Photo from Mrs. Daube, California State Capitol Museum Collection

Governor Pardee's Main Office as a museum, 1982.   Photo by Lynn Marlowe, California State Capitol Museum

ments found under the floor of the podium furnished clues for reconstruction of the ceiling.

By 1862, the number of Assemblymen in the legislature had grown to 80. The Constitution of 1879 set the Assembly at that number.

The Museum Rooms: Each of the executive office/museum rooms presents a dramatic scene, as if at any moment State officials might return and resume duties. Furnishings and events depicted are accurate in every detail. Some 10,000 items went into recreating the rooms.

Governor George Pardee's three room suite of offices: In Pardee's office newspapers and telegrams bring news of the disaster. When Pardee heard of the earthquake, April 18, 1906, he immediately wired San Francisco officials, pledging aid. By noon, he had ordered 3,400 National Guard troops to San Francisco, Oakland, Santa Rosa, and San Jose.

Pardee had gained a reputation as a cautious, procrastinating administrator. Perhaps his medical training enabled him to act decisively in the emergency.

Since San Francisco was cut off by the catastrophe, Pardee set up offices in Oakland. Before the Gover-

nor's return to Sacramento, he had taken charge of sanitary regulations in San Francisco and declared a bank holiday until safes and vaults could be opened. With the aid of his wife, he disbursed $4 million in food and gifts and $1 million in cash.

Pardee wired the California delegation in Washington, urging them to press payment of claims on the federal government, some dating back to the Civil War. Congress settled for $46 million. He also called a special session of the legislature to enact relief measures.

The furnishings in his office include both originals and reproductions. The two main desks were in Pardee's original office. One was found, topped with modern material, in a state office. The massive bookcases are reproductions. The burgundy velvet draperies at the windows flow on the floor in an arrangement called "pooling."

The bouquet of yellow and white flowers show painstaking attention to detail. A few petals have fallen on the table. It duplicates the one in the historic photo used as a re-creation guide.

In the Anteroom, a State Capitol Commission

Governor Pardee's Office. Note lincrusta wainscot, the "pooling" of the velvet draperies.   *Photo by Leonard McKay*

Governor Pardee's Anteroom. This photo was used to create the museum anteroom. Pardee is on the far right.

Photo from Pardee Home Foundation, circa 1906

meeting is interrupted during a discussion of the 1906 remodeling. Luckily, Capitol Commissioners signed $30,000 in bids before the 1906 earthquake caused inflated prices and shortage of materials.

In his small private office, the wainscot is "lincrusta," a linoleum-like wall paper embossed with repeat patterns, in vogue at the turn-of-the-century. Here it is patterned in cream and gold. Applications asking for pardons are on the desk. A state medical text, for which Pardee wrote a chapter on vaccination, illustrates his interests as a medical doctor.

The Secretary of State's Office: Election posters on the walls show this is November 1902, and Charles F. Curry (elected 1898) is running for reelection. Curry's workroom is depicted here. About six employees carried on the Secretary's diverse duties. The hat and coat on the hatrack are of the period, similar to garments that might-have-been-worn by Curry's sister, Minerva. Nepotism was all right, then.

Documents lay on desks, tied with red tape. It's still used by the legislature. The copy press made a

single copy of several letters at a time on tissue sheets. The original correspondence was written or typed, using a special ink that was activated by dampness. The wash basin in the corner half-hidden by a screen was not a luxury, but a necessity. After dipping a pen point in an ink well all day, hands were always messy.

An Oriental rug covers the hardwood floor. In 1899, it was generally thought that carpeting (before vacuum cleaners) was unsanitary. The large desk was actually used by Curry. The clock is original; it had been used at the State Archives. The fireplace mantel was reproduced from one privately owned that matched the original. The stove in front is of the period. The fireplaces never heated adequately, so coal burning stoves were added in 1899.

The room was first assembled as a mock-up in the warehouse and carefully checked against a photograph of the room.

The State Treasurer's Office: State Treasurer Truman Reeves kept the entire money reserves—$7

The museum Treasurer's office of 1906.   *Photo by Lynn Marlowe, 1982, California State Capitol Museum Collection*

million in gold coins—in the 10' x 10' vault in his 1906 office.

The original vault, with a hand-painted scene of Sequoia redwoods on the door, was found in Coloma State Historic Park. Minerva and a grizzly bear head adorn the 7-ton safe, returned from Sutter's Fort. At the turn-of-the-century, the safe was probably kept inside the vault.

Some taxes were paid in gold. State employees could also cash their warrants at the office. Note the canvas money bag. It would have contained 1,000 double eagles, gold coins valued at $20 each, a total of $20,000. Today, one block from the Capitol, the current vault is 400 times the size of the early vault, although it contains only paper—no gold.

Note the rare Renaissance revival table and the porcelain cuspidor. The cuspidor was *de rigueur* in the offices of the time—and even in fashionable Victorian parlors.

Next door, a single room, featuring a 100-foot square vault of the 1930's, represents growth and consequent changes in government.

The Attorney General's Office: Attorney General Ulysses G. Webb split his time between his San Francisco office and Sacramento. His assistant, Charles Post worked here. It's May 1906, just after the earthquake, and he is preparing for a special legislative session to enact relief measures.

Post was a lover of roses so a bouquet adorns his office. The stove has been removed for the summer and the chimney hole is covered with a "flue stopper." A collection of law books fills the glassed-in bookcase.

This is the only room for which there was no photo-guide. The furniture is antique, original to the period, and arranged as it might-have-been.

State Library Exhibit Room: This exhibit room recreates the ambience of the 1900-1910 period. At the time the library was housed in the Apse, a semi-circular structure which was razed in 1949.

The mezzanine was a feature of the old library. The periodical rack is original. The "cabinet of curiosities," might have come directly from the old reading room.

Donna Penwell, part of the museum staff, assembled

Treasurer's office in 1898. This photo was used to create Truman Reeves office in 1906 for the museum.

Photo from the California State Treasurer

the collection of 3,000 period volumes, none dated past 1910, largely from local bookstores. Photos of the Capitol over the years are of special interest.

Archives Exhibit Room: The blue and pink hues of the ceiling and frieze were found preserved behind an air duct in another room. The plasterwork designs were recreated from the original ceiling. It is a masterpiece of old time arts of parget, stenciling, and hand-painting.

The room houses a changing exhibit of original documents from the State Archives.

Exhibit Room: The basement exhibit room furnishes a quick way to gain an understanding of building techniques, changes in government, and the Capitol's history.

Among the exhibits is a ledger that tells a compelling story of growth and change. The Department of Motor Vehicles started out in 1905, as one desk, one clerk, and a ledger. The clerk wrote applicants' names in the ledger and mailed out chauffeur's badges. Contrast that with today when the department has branches in every county, a large staff, and computers.

Reproductions of Reuben Clark's architectural drawings for the original building and his watercolor conception of the finished Capitol are on exhibit.

The original mast that supported the gold ball had been on display in the State Archives. Weathered and deteriorating, it was replaced in 1952.

When the mast was replaced, foreman Frank Bodah and his workmen enclosed notes in a bottle and fastened it to the lower lip of the ball. The Secretary of State, the Treasurer, the State Architect signed a document, and wrapped it in foil for future generations to find. It was reminiscent of the original ceremony that took place in 1871.

A final question to be answered: What was the cost?

The estimate in 1975 was $42 million, to be finished in three years. Nobody knew what the restoration involved—its scope and complexity. Delays and inflation boosted the cost to $59 million by 1979.

After six years, the cost at completion, 1982, was over $67 million—approximately $3 for every man, woman and child in California.

How can comparisons be made when the project is unique? State office space costs $85 to $100 a square

Attorney General Ulysses G. Webb's recreated office.   *Photo by Leonard McKay*

State Library Exhibit Room. Recreated stairs to the mezzanine.   *Photo by Leonard McKay*

foot to build. Costs to restore the Capitol ran about $315 a square foot. Comparison of the two, however, is like comparing a rooster to a peacock.

Complaints of extravagance circulated while the Capitol was being restored. Now, that it is finished, the Capitol holds almost everyone spellbound by its spectacular beauty.

The people who worked on it loved it.

Patty Blaha McLaren, employed by Welton Becket, gave her reason, "I don't think of myself as a secretary, typist, or receptionist. I'm a person that's involved in restoration of the State Capitol. You can't work here and not get into it.... Most of us kept scrapbooks. It's going to be a hard act to follow for everyone."

The team of architects, engineers, contractors, and historical consultants worked exceptionally well together despite differing viewpoints. Hundreds of decisions as to how and what was to be done were discussed in weekly meetings. The men and women argued "like the devil." The end result was that alternate methods were considered, analyzed, and the most efficient chosen. At times, controversy had to be solved with realistic compromise. Differences were like those within a family, since everyone was working for the same goals.

The new/old Capitol meets these goals admirably. Thirty thousand tons of reinforced concrete enables the structure "to ride the waves like a concrete ship." John Worsley vouches that the Capitol will withstand an earthquake measuring 7.5 on the Richter scale. Museum rooms and the downstairs exhibit room preserve the past and showcase change and growth in government.

Safety, practicality, and beauty combine in the preservation of a historical landmark, a source of pride, inspiration, and education for today and the future.

The majestic dome of the Capitol rises above terraced grounds. Circa 1920.   *California State Library, 1920*

CHAPTER II
Capitol Park
A Setting to Match the Capitol

Without the park, the Capitol would be like a diamond without a setting. Together, park and building qualify as the nation's most beautiful State Capitol. The 40-acre arboretum is famous for its 40,000 trees, shrubs, and flowers.

After restoration, the areas immediately around the Capitol needed replanting. Dan Johnson, State Landscape Architect, says, "We didn't want to draw attention from the Capitol. We wanted to keep it simple, and keep a historic look. Shrubs near the building had to be background for colorful flowers."

Victorians favored palms for their exotic feathery foliage. Two varieties, the Senegal date palm and fan palms, will reach the first ledge of the building. Star and saucer magnolia, flowering dogwoods, rhododendrons, and Oregon grape will furnish background along with seasonal bloom.

Trees and shrubs from every continent and climate seem to thrive almost side by side in the park. "They might not flourish as well as in their native habitat," says James DeJournett, Associate Landscape Architect, "but they survive very well. Trees sensitive to frost, like the jacaranda, grow in a microclimate protected by huge camphor trees."

All the greenery acts as foil for camellias, roses, and varied flower beds.

The camellia is a legacy from the Chinese who brought them to California when they came to mine gold and build the transcontinental railroad. The two-acre grove started in 1953, when the Native Daughters of the Golden West donated 176 shrubs to the park, each dedicated to a pioneer Californian.

Among today's 300 camellias is the $5000 "Pink Perfection," willed to the State by a San Jose woman so it would have good care. Her heirs sprayed the

Hundreds of camellia bushes bloom in the late winter and early spring on the grounds.   *Photo by Leonard McKay*

Many varieties of palm trees adorn the Capitol grounds.
Photo by Leonard McKay

leaves with paraffin to retain moisture, and transported it to Sacramento by flatbed truck at a cost of just over $5000.

The park regularly donates camellia blossoms to the Camellia Festival, held each year in February-March. It also gives cut camellias to other non-profit organizations—8,755 blooms in 1982.

The Capitol gardens are one of 12 experimental rose gardens in the nation. The American Rose Society, made up of rose growers, provides several hundred new roses each year. They arrive identified by number only; names follow six months later. The state gets the roses free. In turn, rose growers see which plants "test out" and put these into production.

The roses glow in a spectacular show of pinks, yellows, and reds. From this spot, one can stand still and identify over 50 different varieties of trees, including eucalyptus, pine, fir, maple, cypress, and chestnut. The rose garden has become a favorite place for weddings with one, sometimes two, on Saturdays. There is no fee—all that is required is a permit.

Today's rose garden site was once intended for the Governor's mansion. The legislature appropriated $50,000 for construction and bought the land for $14,000. Work on the three-story mansion commenced, but was unfinished for many years due to lack of funds. When Governor Newton Booth refused to live in it, the legislature changed its function to the State Printing Office (1875). By 1923, the weight of

The cactus garden is located on the southeast corner of the grounds. Many varieties show the various forms of cactus.
Photo by Leonard McKay

the presses had ruined the floors and the building was demolished.

The cactus garden represents the California desert. Hundreds of school children sent the plants to Governor Johnson in 1914. The sculptured shapes of some 25 varieties complement each other. Requiring little water, they reign alone except for the state flower, the California poppy. Its satiny orange flowers blaze against the gray-green cactus. Their feathery green foliage dies back in winter, while the cactus stays the same year around.

Where cactus grows now, was the site of the State Fair from 1875 to 1905. In those days, California was most importantly an agricultural state, and winning a blue ribbon for wine, cheese, or an agricultural product was a matter for great pride. Exhibits were housed in an elaborate pinnacled pavilion that looked like a cross between a castle and a greenhouse, belonging to the State Agricultural Society. Banners flying from slender towers, the flag unfurled atop the dome, a fountain, and plantings—still to grow—gave a festive air. The fair was a lively social occasion, a place to renew old acquaintances, as well as a chance for the blue ribbon.

Providing continuous color for 25 flowerbeds throughout the park is an exercise in logistics, requiring advance planning. Tulip bulbs, for instance, are imported from Holland, so must be ordered in February and March for spring display over a year away.

"The first step is developing a color scheme," explains DeJournett. "Next year we're using a combination of dark purple tulips with a light shade; it should be dramatic. Each year we do something different. If we score spectacular success, we may repeat it but in a new area. Ranunculus put on quite a show. I'll also feature "Texas," a yellow daffodil with a double orange throat."

Seeds, too, must be ordered ahead, planted in the nursery and be ready to shift into beds for a succession of color. New beds have to be planted before the old one looks bedraggled.

Each bed is rototilled, rejuvenated with soil nutrients and replanted twice a year. Much thought is given to the design and color of individual planting areas and to the overall effect.

Throughout the park groves and statues commemorate the men who gave their lives on battlefields. Scenic Memorial Grove, a gift in 1897 from the Ladies of the Grand Army of the Republic of California and Nevada remembers Union veterans of the Civil War. The 1958 *Blue Book* lists the trees, planted as saplings from famous battlefields: sugar maple (Ball's Bluff), pitch pine (Chickamauga), silver maple (Chattanooga), locust (Spottsylvania Courthouse), box elder (Missionary Ridge and Lookout Mountain),

pencil cedar (Cold Harbor), scarlet maple (Chancellorsville and Franklin), sand blackjack oak (Kenesaw Mountain), American elm (Winchester, Wilderness and Gettysburg), white oak (Vicksburg), winged elm (Melvern Hill), tulip tree (Five Forks), and black walnut (Seven Pines). Memorial services take place here annually.

Nearby, a statue of a soldier of the Spanish American War stands above the trout pond. Each spring, after the pool is cleaned, the American River Hatchery restocks the pool with 50 fingerlings, 8 to 12 inches long. By the end of the season, the trout weigh 4 to 5 pounds and are put back in the American River. The cycle is repeated. Occasionally, groundsmen find antennae attached to fishlines in the bushes, evidence of "midnight fishermen." The pool's waterfall resembles a crystal-glass sheet. Groundskeeper Bill Grund, leader of park walks, knows the reason for the waterfalls smooth flow: "It's flowing over a bullet-proof piece of glass taken off the chief-of-police's desk, while he was out of the office."

A Chinese elm was dedicated as a Freedom tree in 1972, to the memory of POWS and those missing in action in the Vietnam War.

A reproduction of the Liberty Bell, cast in France,

The bronze statue of Fr. Junipero Serra stands above a relief map showing the missions he established in California. Behind the statue are beautiful camellia gardens.

Photo by Leonard McKay

and the bell from the U.S.S. *California*, the only battleship built on the Pacific coast, are next to the trout pond.

The impressive bronze statue of Father Junipero Serra rises above a relief map of California, showing the missions he established.

Across the park, a valley oak and grinding stones recognizes our heritage from the early Indians.

Grounds keepers are instructed to cut the thirty pound cones off the Australian tree, *Araucaria bidwilli*. Grund's eyes twinkle, "It's popularly called the Bunga-bunga tree. I don't know how that translates, but it's probably what the aborigines yell when a cone falls on their heads."

About the monkey tree, Grund jokes, "Even a monkey, looking at that bunch of tails, can't tell where one leaves off and another begins. It's a puzzlement."

Some of the older trees are feeling their age. They've had such good care that they've outlived their normal life spans. "We often make cuttings of declining trees and plant them nearby to preserve historical integrity," says Grund.

There is much history in the park. After the flooding of 1860-61, the Capitol was raised 13 feet above ground level. Workers hauled in river silt in horse-drawn wagons. Only one and one half yards could be hauled per trip, so it took 61,000 trips to fill the grounds to street level.

Many of the trees today date back to the first planting of 800 trees in 1870-71. The line of magnificent deodar cedars at the west front, for example. Tiny deodars from high in the Himalaya Mountains in India were dug up, boxed, and shipped to San Francisco by sailing vessels. From there they were transferred to river steamers. Horse-drawn wagons hauled them from Sacramento's dock to the Capitol. Cost was $2 per tree.

The stone pines, grown from seed from Italy; the redwoods; the native Washingtonia palms on the park's perimeter; the immense Southern magnolias; and tulip trees are either original plantings or very old.

Roller skates have become an institution enjoying the wide walks and jumping the steps.   *Photo by Leonard McKay*

Squirrels are a park institution.   *Photo by Leonard McKay*

The first plantings were in formal straight lines in harmony with the classic architecture. After 1880, trees were clumped in natural groupings.

The double curving row of English elms backed by fan palms marks the old driveway for carriages and exercising horses. "Back in Sacramento's early days it was a fashionable gathering spot," says Grund. "People would get in their surreys every Sunday afternoon to drive around the track and visit friends."

By 1905 the identity of many of the trees had been lost. In that year, Alice Eastwood, Head of the Horticultural Department of the Academy of Sciences, San Francisco, went over the entire Park. Each tree was labeled with its common name, botanical name, and country of origin. The same procedure is followed today.

The terraced grounds surrounded by an ornamental iron fence with massive granite gateposts remained until 1954. With completion of the East Annex, the terraces were recontoured in a gentle slope to the street and the decorative fence removed.

Capitol Park is "on stage" at all times with a constant audience of visitors.

How is the meticulous maintenance managed? Eight groundskeepers are assigned full time to the park. Additionally, other "support people" who work in the greenhouses or on other state grounds are "pulled" to the Capitol gardens as needed. This ensures efficient utilization of manpower, yet allows for extra help in planting and pruning. Pruning, particularly, requires expertise. Towering trees, such as the 135 foot tall English elms, require scaling spurs for climbing and safety nets as well as pruning equipment. All employees are under civil service and must pass written and oral exams.

The entire park has a sprinkler system, installed over the years. Some of the old copper pipes require constant maintenance. Lawns are kept green and fit by surface fertilizing three to four times a year, using six to eight tons of fertilizer, varied according to nutrient requirements and season.

Beady-eyed fox squirrels are both bane and asset to the park. The furry creatures adore sharpening their teeth on the plastic plaques that identify trees and nibbling on sprinkler heads.

By now, the squirrels are a park institution. Any move to eliminate them would be followed by a loud outcry. So, instead, park officials try to slow the damage by feeding the squirrels almonds and walnuts, contributed by local companies in 100 pound sacks. A band of "regulars," also, feed the squirrels. They're featured in many a photo and loved by the children. DeJournett gives compelling testimony for squirrel-appeal, "Legislators like to have their pictures taken with the capitol squirrels just before elections."

Above all, the park is a people's park—all ages and all people.

Smartly dressed women and men—with briefcases—quickstep through the Capitol doors. A derelict stretches out on the lawn; time passes him by. At the west entrance, demonstrators harangue an audience that responds with wild gestures and shrill voices. Demonstrations can be mild, also, merely a sign-carrying walk back and forth. High school bands play for anyone that listens. Once a year, the Sacramento Symphony Orchestra gives a finished performance on capitol grounds.

Benches throughout the park are an invitation to sit and look about. Youngsters rollerskate; oldsters meditate. School children with a quota of teachers and parents lunch from brown bags. Probably, they have carpooled for their visit to the Capitol. Secretaries from nearby offices eat and sun, too.

Tourists come from close by and faraway. Cameras click as people pose by cactus, bells, and olive trees or on the Capitol steps.

The media is an almost constant presence. A full television crew films a newsworthy event. Perhaps, a single young woman interviews a legislator under a tree for a news spot or talk show.

Yet, in the midst of the vibrating action, there is a

sense of tranquility. The trees, with their network of branches overhead, have deep roots. They grew through years of yesterdays and will be here through years of tomorrow.

California's pioneers envisioned spacious gardens to match the splendor of their Capitol. If they could see Capitol Park in its maturity, they would know their optimistic visions became reality.

Tall trees form a background for the Capitol.   *Photo by Leonard McKay*

CHAPTER III
The Capitol
A Continued Story

On January 4 1982, the legislators opened sessions in their redecorated chambers and the doors of the Capitol were reopened to the public.

The most "impressive restoration work in America" was honored by the most impressive, week-long Gala Celebration in America.

It began with ribbon cutting ceremonies at noon. Hundreds of people gathered in the rotunda to feast on a five-foot high 500-pound cake with white frosting constructed as a replica of the Capitol. Living history pageants, outdoor concerts, a special performance of the Sacramento Symphony Orchestra, and a Gala Command Performance of the Stars were scheduled during the week.

There was a special reception open only to those who worked on the restoration, and a private white-tie Gala Ball for legislators and dignitaries. On January 9th, a parade marched around historic Capitol Park and formal dedication services were held on the west steps. The $600,000 celebration—paid for with private funds—ended with the largest fireworks ever, showering sparks on the Capitol dome.

Several projects had to be completed before the Capitol restoration could be considered finished. Most of the statues on the parapet were taken down in the 1906 remodeling. They were assigned to storage "just in case someone wants them back." Where did they go? The mystery of the vanishing statues has never been solved. The other four had deteriorated and were taken down during the renovation of the 1950's.

Four of the larger than life statues have been recreated and installed on the parapet. Flanking the west portico, an Indian warrior on horseback fends off a grizzly; and also on horseback, an Indian maiden undergoes a buffalo attack. In their former positions, two Grecian women hold symbols of the federal government, the state seal, and the state constitution. They symbolize the nation's states rejoining the Union. Historical consultant, Raymond Girvigian, says, "They are earthquake proof, firmly reinforced and tied to the building."

The question of whether to return the statue of Queen Isabella of Spain to the rotunda center caused a tempest in Capitol corridors.

The statue graced its gray granite base from 1883, when pioneer banker, D. O. Mills, gave it to the state, until removed for the restoration.

Architect John Worsley admitted, "Historically, it should be there, but architecturally, it should never have been in the rotunda." He contended, "The statue disrupts traffic flow, and furthermore, was never designed to be viewed in the round."

Senator James R. Mills demurred, "I don't see how we can call this a historical restoration if we left it out. It's an extremely fine piece of work by a noted American sculptor."

The completed renovated Capitol with statues returned to the parapet.

The glistening white marble statue was returned to its traditional position in the rotunda on Columbus Day, 1982.

The Arthur Mathews murals, depicting phases of California history, have been placed in their own rotunda in the basement.

"The response of the public has been overwhelming," says John Kolb, Director of the Capitol Museum. "There were 95,594 people on 4,068 tours the first four months. There were also 960 reserved groups." Uncounted are the people who wander on self-guided tours.

School classes have flocked in by the bus load, by car pool, and chartered bus on overnight tours from farther away. They tour the Capitol, see the museum exhibits, an orientation film, and talk to their legislators or the legislator's aides. Their cameras and memories record the event.

"The students come away very aware that the Capitol belongs to them and they can have a voice in government," said one teacher from Los Angeles.

Carefully selected tour guides receive two weeks of formal training. "They study the Capitol inside out, getting teaching and advice from the Capitol staff," says Pauline Grenbeaux Spear, visitor services supervisor.

Californians have always had free and easy access to their Capitol. The policy of a "people's Capitol" continues. You're free to wander about. Free to watch the legislature at work whenever they are in session.

There is a choice of tours. For history buffs, the Historic Tour steps inside the turn-of-the-century Museum Rooms. The Restored Capitol Tour emphasizes the restoration itself, along with information on state history, architecture, and the legislative process. Tours for school classes and other groups, by reservation only, place their emphasis on the legislative process. For up-to-date-tour information call the California State Capitol Museum.

A basement cafeteria, open to the public, serves a variety of foods at affordable prices. In the dining area, salvaged bricks are utilized in partitions and a series of graceful arches, spanning the ceiling. Printouts of bills to be considered by the legislature are available in the downstairs bill room. Nearby, the bookstore carries books relating to the Capitol and California history.

The Capitol promises to become one of Sacramento's biggest tourist attractions. It's been suggested that admission be charged to recoup reconstruction costs. Richard Ross, former administrative officer of the Joint Rules Committee, reacts with one word, "Outrageous!"

"If there's one place that ought to be open to the public, it's the Capitol. The public has paid for it—dearly. Why would we want to charge people to come through their own building?"

The new/old Capitol is strong, beautiful, and settled-down, ready to serve the people—if properly maintained—for another 100 years.

Queen Isabella of Spain returns to the rotunda center.
Photo by Leonard McKay

The new cafeteria is on the same lower level as the museum theatre and bookstore. It is open to the general public.
Photo by Leonard McKay

Carefully selected tour guides deftly describe the old and the reconstructed Capitol.   *Photo by Leonard McKay*

"If there's one place that ought to be open to the public, it's the Capitol. The public has paid for it—dearly. Why would we want to charge people to come through their own building?"

The new/old Capitol is strong, beautiful, and settled-down, ready to serve the people—if properly maintained—for another 100 years.

CHAPTER IV
The Beginning
The Convention Fails to Select a Permanent Capital

In the beginning, California's capital was far-and-away from settled-down. For five years, the capital wandered, as restless as a miner chasing rumors of gold. Citizens dubbed it "the Capital on wheels." Even after the capital settled in Sacramento, the legislature debated and cities continued to maneuver for capital status. Connivers for the capital thrived at the Constitutional Convention.

Impatient Californians adopted a constitution in 1849 and established a state government without waiting for the federal government's blessing.

The reason behind California's abrupt leap into statehood lies in one word: Gold!

One morning James Marshall, eccentric carpenter and boss at Sutter's sawmill on the American River, noticed a few flakes of glinting gold in the ditch for millstream runoff. Marshall became so excited that he could never quite remember the date. A Mormon employee (and poor speller), Henry Bigler, wrote in his pocket diary: "January 24, 1848, This day some kind of mettle was found in the tail race that looks like goald first discovered by James Martial, the Boss of the Mill."

The discovery of gold generated revolutionary changes in California. Shock waves vibrated outward around the world, like an earthquake of tremendous magnitude, jolting into motion an avalanche of one hundred thousand fortune seekers, the greatest migration in human history.

Nine days after Marshall's momentous discovery, the signing of the Treaty of Guadalupe Hidalgo with Mexico signaled United States possession of California.

The conquest ended; but the combination military-alcalde government of the conquest continued. The Hispanic system, with the alcalde (mayor) responsible for a wide range of decisions, sufficed in the pastoral rancho life of the Californios. Under the chaotic conditions and pressures of the gold rush it was clearly inadequate. Disdainful Americans called it the "no government." No courts, no jury, no code of laws, no jail, no clear land titles, no binding contracts.

The thirtieth Congress, deadlocked over the complex question of slavery, fearful that recognition of California would upset the fragile balance of slave and free states maintained since 1820, failed to enact a territorial bill.

The information reached California in December 1848. Widespread dissatisfaction flamed in a sequence of meetings in San José, Sacramento, Monterey, and Sonoma. All concurred in the need for the people to form a government for security from spiraling crime and protection of property.

At this point, Brevet General Bennett Riley arrived to relieve Colonel Richard Mason and assume the office of Governor and Commanding General. Mason relinquished his duties eagerly with the parting advice, "Call a convention to form either a territorial or state government." Riley had served many years on the frontier and won distinction on the battlefield.

Captain Thomas Fallon raised the first American flag over the Mexican Juzgado (Court House) at San José in July 1846.
San José was a Mexican Pueblo of over a hundred adobe dwellings when the Americans arrived.   Leonard McKay Collection

He had every intention of "obeying orders" and continuing the legal military government. After experiencing existing conditions for several weeks, he wisely changed his mind.

Gold-crazed young men converged on San Francisco with accelerating immigration expected. The city, grown to 9,000 inhabitants, boasted 46 gambling joints, 48 brothels, and 537 saloons. "Ghost ships" crowded her harbor as entire crews deserted for the mines. Already citizens had formed a "legislative assembly" to replace the alcalde government.

In Monterey, soldiers deserted for the placers, except for a few faithful officers. The General ground his own coffee and prepared his own mess. Men posted for sentinel duty disappeared inside of fifteen minutes, "musket and all." The gruff 55-year-old general felt increasingly powerless.

On May 28, 1849, the United States steamer, *Edith*, brought news that Congress had adjourned March 3rd without providing for territorial government. However, the Senate had passed a bill extending revenue laws over California. Anger erupted, "Congress has assumed the right to tax us without

representation, to tax us without giving us any government at all."

When General Riley received the news, he put already formulated plans in operation. On June 3rd, he issued a proclamation calling for an election and detailing requirements for a Constitutional Convention to meet at Monterey, September 1, 1849.

The 48 delegates—Spanish elite, roughhewn frontiersmen, polished Southern gentlemen, ex-military men, "old settlers" who spoke English with Mexican accents, and new comers—reflected the diversity of California. For six weeks the men worked—"disputed like the devil at home"—but always in an atmosphere of good humor and intelligent compromise that deepened friendship. The constitution they forged served California well for 30 years—with one exception.

The failure to settle on a definite capital site became a source of trouble and squabbling for years.

The location of the capital was one of the last issues considered by the convention. Mindful of the economic advantages, San José citizens urged their delegates to quietly canvass the convention as to the *pueblo's* chances. "Old settlers" James Reed and Charles White galloped to Monterey to lobby and support their representatives.

Colton Hall, Monterey: The Constitutional Convention adopted a Constitution for California, but failed to establish a permanent seat of government.
Photo from California State Library

A committee presented the proposal: the first legislature would meet in San José as the permanent capital, subject to approval by two-thirds of the legislators.

Captain H. W. Halleck offered a compromise: Monterey for the first session: subsequent sessions to be held at San José. He reasoned Monterey already had a building. Also, the government archives could not be moved until legalized by the legislature.

Halleck's logical arguments had merit. Colton Hall was the only building in all California suitable for a State House. Its 30' x 70' upper floor had served the Convention delegates admirably. Alcalde Walter Colton had constructed the town hall/schoolhouse out of local chalkstone (Carmel stone) at practically no cost. He utilized the "labor of convicts, taxes on rum, and the banks of gamblers," and more than a little inguenuity. Besides, the former capital of Alta California possessed a crescent-shaped bay and crisp, invigorating climate.

San José representatives, K. H. Dimmick and J. D. Hoppe, countered: San José was the true center of California. Affluent citizens had already donated 31 to 32 acres for the proposed capitol grounds,

60 lots worth $1,000 apiece. A suitable building neared completion.

Charles Botts argued that access, not precise geographic location, was the deciding factor. Reached by sea and land Monterey was accessible to the greatest number of people. He predicted the capital would move frequently to accommodate shifting population and improved transportation.

R. M. Price, though unauthorized by his constituents, made a bid for San Francisco as navigation, commercial, and population center.

Henry Tefft offered beautiful Mission San Luis Obispo.

Robert Semple, convention president and founder of Benicia, boasted of its commercial possibilities but made it clear he had nothing to give away. "I have lots there which the Government can have by paying for them; and they can also have a building there very soon provided they build it on those lots after they have paid for them."

O. M. Wozencraft put forth Stockton as the head of ship navigation. José M. Covarrubias favored Santa Barbara both for its location and its salubrious climate.

William Gwin and L. W. Hastings supported San José. Hastings was of the opinion: "The people of Monterey have had it here quite long enough; unless, indeed, we are to be governed altogether by time-honored custom." It was a compelling argument; Americans wanted to change—not follow—Hispanic customs.

San José's well-planned efforts and promises had won the capital—at least for the present (21 ayes, 14 noes).

On the day of adjournment, Riley issued a proclamation setting the election for November 13, 1848, only a month away. Immediately, he dispatched proclamation, constitution, and W. M. Steuart's *Address to the People of California* to the San Francisco office of *Alta California* for printing. Within a week 8,000 copies in English and 2,000 in Spanish were on their way to the ranchos, towns, and mining camps from San Diego to the Oregon line.

Candidates campaigned actively, traveling by horseback with blankets tied behind, talking and handshaking wherever they found a small group. At night they found shelter in a miner's tent or spread their blankets under trees. It was a rugged campaign made harder by the rainy season. The short time and scattered camps made it possible to reach only a small percentage of voters.

In his *Memoirs*, Peter Burnett recalled some of his experiences in reaching the miners' vote when running for governor. At Mud Springs, he found sleeping quarters in a large canvas-tent hotel. A severe storm came up in the night collapsing the tent. Until daylight the future governor stood hugging the center tent pole trying to keep dry under the flapping canvas.

Inured by previous mishaps, Burnett kept calm during a speech at Portsmouth Square. He spoke to the immense crowd from a six-foot-high platform of rough boards supported by scantlings. Well into his speech, the platform gave way and fell to the ground except for the small portion on which he stood. Burnett calmly forged ahead, "Though others might fall, I will be sure to stand."

On election day, torrential rains kept many miners from the polls—others were just apathetic. They had come to California to strike it rich and return home; later they would change their minds. Some voted only for those they knew or knew about. Bayard Taylor tells of a miner who followed a different approach:

Great Seal of California.   *Photo from California State Library*

I went it blind in coming to California and I'm not going to stop now. I voted for the Constitution, and I've never seen the Constitution, I voted for all candidates, and I don't know a dammed one of them. I'm going it blind all through I am.

Of the 76,000 Americans, only one-sixth voted. The vote favored the Constitution overwhelmingly—12,065 for, 811 against.

Peter Burnett, Governor-elect, became known politically through participation in meetings agitating for state government. In 1848 he led the first wagon party of gold seekers from Oregon. His status as a family man with six children, two of them daughters of marriageable age, contributed to his election. Burnett won by a large majority: 6,716 votes with 3,185 for his nearest rival.

Former Convention member John McDougal was elected Lieutenant-Governor. Edward Gilbert, editor of *Alta California*, and George Wright were sent as representatives to United States Congress. Voters also elected state senators and representatives to the first legislature, meeting at San José on December 15, 1849.

Surprisingly, few of the men who had served in the Constitutional Convention went on to the first legislature.

CHAPTER V
Legislature of a Thousand Drinks
First Session: 1849-1850

The legislators traveled to San José by horseback, *carreta* (a hidebound cart resembling a topless bird-cage with wooden wheels), steamer, and stagecoach under uncomfortable, dangerous, even life-threatening conditions.

Violent rains beat down relentlessly. Roads—more aptly trails—churned into treacherous bogs. A six-mile lake stretched from the Embarcadero of Alviso to the Pueblo of San José. Muddy streets harbored puddles, deep as ponds. A little boy drowned in one at the corner of First and Santa Clara Streets.

In Sacramento, Dr. Logan's rain gauge recorded upward of 36 inches of continuous rain, October 28, 1849 to March 22, 1850. (Normal rainfall measured 14 inches.)

A near shipwreck threatened to capsize the smooth course of government. A majority of the senators, ten or twelve assemblymen and Lieutenant Governor-elect McDougal booked passage for the Embarcadero on the small steamer *Mint*. Three hours out of San Francisco, a gale came up; storm-blasted waves bludgeoned the small steamer. Fearful of capsizing, the crew panicked and prepared to abandon ship. Passengers froze—terror stricken.

Selim E. Woodworth, who had resigned his commission in the Navy for the Senate, sprang to the wheel. Sternly, he ordered the cowering engineer and fireman, "Back to your stations." He reassured the passengers, "There's hope unless the ship overturns in changing course."

In turning, the vessel shipped water, flooding cabins, but passengers landed safely at San Francisco.

Understandably, most passengers continued to the capital by stagecoach overland. Short of funds, Assemblyman-elect John Bigler and his family proceeded by steamer. The next day, "The bay in perfect repose," they reached the Embarcadero without incident.

When the legislature convened, December 15, 1849, only six senators and fourteen assemblymen had arrived. Without a quorum both houses adjourned until December 17. Military Governor Riley and State Secretary Halleck came on Sunday. Governor-elect Burnett arrived by *carreta*. By Monday most of the sixteen senators and thirty-six assemblymen, mud-spattered and bedraggled, had straggled in.

Disappointed, tired legislators growled their dissatisfaction over the adobe capitol building. Resembling a graceless unfinished crate, the 60' x 40' upper-story housed the assembly. The lower floor was divided into a Senate Chamber 40' x 20', an office for the Secretary of State, and rooms for committee meetings.

Until completion of their quarters, the Senate met in pioneer Isaac Branham's front parlor on the southwest side of the plaza.

When James Reed and Charles White had captured the capital, the back-clapping and congratulations soon turned to second thoughts. "How in heaven's name could San José deliver the promised building— in two months?"

Pueblo de San José de Guadalupe, California's first civil settlement, had been founded by José Moraga in 1777. The once drowsy *pueblo*, aroused by the gold rush, now bustled as a trade center. Already, "back-wash" from the mines overflowed in tents and shacks, hiding the "huddle of adobes." It had doubled in size and suffered acute growing pains since the decision to make it a capital. Lumber, when obtain-able, went for $500 per 1,000 feet; labor, also short, for $16 a day.

Providentially, Pierre Sansevain and Zepheryn Rochon had nearly completed the building they intended for a hotel. The *Ayuntamiento* (city coun-cil) agreed to an exorbitant rent of $4,000 a month, then decided outright purchase for $34,000 made bet-ter sense.

The *pueblo* had no money; Sansevain and Rochon adamantly refused credit. In the crisis, nineteen well-heeled citizens, reluctant to see the "pristine glories attendant on the presence of the Legislature to San José glide from them;" signed a note at eight percent interest a month, a whopping ninety-six percent a year. Joseph Aram, Josiah Belden, and James Reed executed the deed in trust for the above citizens, pro-perty to be conveyed to the *pueblo* on payment.

A visiting Englishman, William Kelly, looked in on the sessions in disdain:

> The senate is a large ill-lighted, badly ventilated room, with a low ceiling, and a rough railing inside the door, beyond which none but the elect may pass. Each member had a rush-bot-tomed arm-chair and a small desk with statio-nery...At the farther end the Speaker is perched in a species of pulpit. The floor is covered with a number of little carpets of various shapes and patterns, looking as if every member con-tributed a patch to make up the robe, which had quite a mosaic appearance. The idea of antiq-uity being assisted by the threadbare state of the whole...The upper floor occupied by the Assembly has the advantage of greater loft-iness and exhibits at once the difference of grade between the common chairs, flat deal tables, and a strip of matting down where the feet are erroneously supposed to rest...

The first legislature has been much criticized for its extreme informality. For the most part members dressed much like miners in flannel shirts, flop hats, boots and the inevitable India rubber coat against the rain. Legislators may have been cleaner than miners, but even that is doubtful given mud and laun-dry problems.

Of course, a few legislators wore dress suits and plug hats. Over two-thirds of the assemblymen never made an appearance without knives or pistols or both," reported Stephen J. Field of the Judiciary

Committee in 1851. "At the same time he removed his hat, he deposited his pistol in his desk drawer."

Under pioneer conditions exacerbated by the gold rush, formality could hardly be expected.

Actually, clothing was practical for a time when streets were bottomless mires. Sidewalks were absent. Cattle and horses roamed the town unre-stricted. Californios dug adobe from the plaza, leav-ing yawning pits. Hundreds of ground squirrels, multiplying rapidly as settlers killed snakes and coyotes, found residence in the plaza. The first city council of San José launched a clean-up campaign, passing an ordinance against digging adobe or skin-ning cattle in the plaza.

Conduct of the legislature matched the informality of dress and surroundings. Kelly, when he visited the State House vividly described his impressions of the proceedings:

> There was no order of debate or system of discussion, but a turbulent dinning colloquy, made up of motions, interruptions, assertions, and contradictions; several members generally on their legs at the same time, and those with legs on the tables, adding to the tumult by the music of their heels. I never could catch the faintest idea of the subject under considera-tion, nor is it possible that the merits of any measure can be sifted under such a species of discussion. They meet about ten o'clock A. M. and are let loose for dinner at one o'clock, when they come out with a rush, like so many over-grown schoolboys. It is unnecessary to add, that smoking, chewing, and whittling, do not constitute an infraction of the rules of either house: privileges that are accorded also to a squad of slipshod clerks or messengers who loll about the stores, making a *tout ensemble* really unique, and entirely characteristic.

Many members were impatient young men, unfamiliar with proper legislative procedures. They

The adobe and frame first Capitol.

were eager to accomplish the business of government and "get back to their moneybags." Other men were stumbling across fortunes on the gold fields or laying the foundations of fortunes as merchants. Many legislators had already established extensive business interests which required supervision.

Service as a legislator required dedication and belief in California's future for it involved personal sacrifice. Small wonder that it was difficult to keep a quorum.

Salaries had been set by the schedule attached to the constitution as $16 per diem with $16 for each twenty miles traveled to and from the capital. Travel pay reflected the high cost of stage coach fare in 1850, $32 or two ounces of gold between San José and San Franciso. Travelers commonly paid their fare with several pinches of gold dust. A pinch, the amount that could be lifted between thumb and a forefinger, was accepted as an ounce worth $16.

Salaries were none too high, particularly since they were paid in state scrip worth 40¢ on the $1. Several resigned when the legislature was barely under way, for they said, "There was nothing in it."

For comparison, the City Council of San José voted themselves a salary of $16, payable in gold coin, actually more than that received by the legislators.

At the time all labor came high priced. Bayard Taylor was amused at "the sight of a burly, long bearded fellow...rubbing a shirt with such violence suds flew and buttons must soon snap off." The washerman with shirts at $8 a dozen easily earned double the wages of a member of the first legislature.

The lawmakers also complained about living conditions. "The lobbyists grabbed the best rooms," they grumbled. "The food is monotonous. Besides prices are exorbitant."

Most politicians crowded into the only hotel. The City Hotel, a one and one-half story frame building on the west side of First Street, charged $5 per day in gold coin for board and lodging. Regularly, boarders stretched their bed rolls on the dining room and barroom floors at $2 the night. At the sound of a Chinese gong, men stampeded for a place at the first table and the best pickings. Despite the scarcity of vegetables, cuisine rated satisfactory. Daily fare: beef, chicken, mutton, wild duck, squirrel and rabbit; potatoes and an occasional onion or egg. Eggs and onions cost 50¢ each.

By February 1850, J. S. Ruckles completed the adobe Mansion House at a cost of $100,000. Its immense fireplace awed the townspeople. Politicians, lulled by the warmth of the blazing fire, chatted about the day's agenda and families left "back home."

For all its expensive stylishness, "wash up" was at the backyard washstand. A fine tooth comb was a necessary item. "If a man scratched his head nobody for a moment thought it was for an idea." Fleas, ubiquitous throughout California, added to the discomfort.

An unpretentious wooden house substituted for an executive mansion for Governor Burnett and his family of six children.

The remainder of the legislators found board and room in private homes. One of these "got up a reputation for battercakes" and was dubbed "Slapjack Hall." Doctor and "Grandma" Bascom arrived in San José on December 10, 1849 by stagecoach "through fearful mud and pouring rain." They found a house "just as good as a corn crib for $7,000" and made four rooms with calico partitions.

Her own story in *Overland Monthly* recounts:

> The first time I knew I had thirteen boarders—
> senators, assemblymen, ministers, and teachers. No one who came would go away....They
> all said they would help in all sorts of ways.
> Mr. Leake [Charles A. Leake, enrolling clerk
> in the Legislature] was a wonderful hand to
> make battercakes. Mr. Bradford [J. Bradford,
> Assemblyman from Sonoma] could brew coffee
> to perfection....

"Grandma" couldn't have managed if her boarders hadn't pitched in. She had six children to care for, too.

She enjoyed her frequent visits to the legislature and observed: "The gentlemen who figured as cooks in my kitchen were the most intelligent and agreeable men....They appeared just as much like gentlemen when they were cooking as when making speeches in the legislature."

Hospitable San Joseans welcomed the legislators to dinners and parties all through the session. Hospitality failed to make up for the weather, their accommodations, and their poverty.

Amidst general dissatisfaction, George Tingley introduced a bill to remove the capital to Monterey on December 19, 1849, even before the Governor's inaugural. The bill passed on the first reading, then was tabled for future action.

Members, who wanted the capital where it would give them the greatest personal advantage, encouraged the grumbling. The fact that the legislators disagreed vociferously favored San José.

When Governor Burnett and Lieutenant Governor McDougal were inaugurated, California's status as a state was nine months away. Yet, Burnett took the oath of office for his two-year term at one o'clock, December 20, 1849:

> I, Peter Burnett do solemnly swear I will support the Constitution of California and will faithfully discharge the duties of the office of Governor to the best of my ability.

In his annual message the next day, Governor Burnett proclaimed California's right to proceed as a self-governing dominion and outlined urgent issues. He assigned priority to adoption of a criminal code, combining the best features of civil and common law. He underscored the unparalleled opportunity to "incorporate the improvements and research and experience others have made."

He also stressed the division of the state into counties, urged laws for the exclusion of Negroes "to avoid their further degradation," and the early appointment of state officers. In conclusion, Burnett predicted, "Either a brillant destiny awaits California or one of the most sordid and degraded... Much will depend on early legislation."

The election of United States Senators at five o'clock that afternoon generated more excitement than the inaugural. The all-important admission of California might very well hinge on the choice of senators and their influence with Congress. Candidates spared no expense in keeping "ranches" (election headquarters) well-stocked with wines, liquors, and cigars. Legislators customarily made daily rounds, quaffing spirits and toasting the candidate's certain success.

John C. Fremont's "ranch" outclassed the rest with twenty-five cases of champagne brought down from his mining property, *Las Mariposas*.

Fremont had chosen not to participate in the Constitutional Convention. At its close, he came forward as a senatorial candidate. An aura of glamour clung to the man journalist Bayard Taylor described as "of medium height, compact figure; thin face, with deep-set eyes, keen as a hawk's." The facile pen of his wife, Jessie, and the oratory of his father-in-law, Senator Benton, broadcasted his accomplishments. His sobriquet of "Pathfinder" and recent participation in the California conquest insured his popularity.

Captain Fremont received the majority, twenty-nine votes on the first ballot. Dr. William Gwin, a seasoned politician with previous experience in Congress, won on the third ballot with a narrow majority of two votes. When they drew lots Gwin won the six year term; Fremont the term for two years.

Governor Burnett's address had set forth essentials to be accomplished as expeditiously as possible to meet urgent needs. Precedents set by other states made definition of duties of state officers relatively simple. The legislators appointed Treasurer, Controller, Attorney General, and Surgeon General as provided by the constitution, successors to be elected.

Eager to get on with their work, the legislature opted for a brief three-day Christmas recess. Impassable roads made it impossible to go home.

San José citizens planned a grand ball to properly

Peter H. Burnett, California's first governor.
California Department of Parks and Recreation

honor the Governor and Legislature, and to raise spirits dampened by the rain-soaked, lonely holiday. Preparations received a setback, when the man in charge absconded with $3,000. Undaunted, citizens raised another $5,000.

Elaborate invitations, printed in gold on pink satin, gave the date: the evening of December 27, 1849, and the place: the Assembly Hall. The countryside was "raked for *señoritas*." Some came by "Lilliputian" steamer from Benicia.

There were no carriages. Guests came on horseback or by oxcart in the midst of a downpour. Governor and Mrs. Burnett, assisted by their two lovely young daughters, Miss Rae and Miss Letitia, received the guests.

General and Mrs. Jessie Fremont, Captain Sutter, and, of course, members of the legislature attended. All the aristocratic Spanish families came: Noriega, Sunol, Pico among them.

The American women wore dainty white dresses with low necklines and ruffled skirts. The Spanish Dons draped serapes over their shoulders. The señoritas wore rebozas they kept on the whole time and smoked *cigaritos*. American ladies exchanged scandalized glances.

Although, the American women's dresses were *au courant*, the señoritas outdid them in vivacity. They swirled in the dance as graceful as tropical butterflies, their red and yellow flannel petticoats peeking from under white skirts.

Language presented difficulties, but a few words, a smile, a flash of the eyes, broke barriers.

At midnight, a delectable repast regaled the guests. Champagne corks popped. There were many toasts to "San José, the capital city."

An incident threatened to mar the gaiety. A Californio, filled with too much spirits, drew out a knife "with gestures wild and reckless." One American seized the knife. Another picked him up "gently" and dropped him down the stairs.

The music, the dancing, the laughter continued "as merry as a marriage ball."

By the first of the year, the lawmakers settled down to setting up a state government "starting from scratch."

The Senate had adopted a motion to print the Governor's message: 1,000 copies in English, 500 copies in Spanish, with an additional 500 copies for presentation to the President and Congress.

The legislature had no money in the treasury to pay for the printing. No money for paper or pen with which to keep minutes, no ink. No money for heating stoves or for salaries. Gold dust from the mines averaged $5,000,000 a month. Yet the state collected nothing on its greatest asset!

Thomas Jefferson Green, the "irrepressible Senator to whom everything was a huge joke," inappropriately headed the Financial Committee. His first bill called for a loan at ten per cent a year. Ridiculous, when the lowest rate was five per cent a month! He reported optimistically: California, not yet admitted to the Union had production "larger than the oldest and richest State...precious metals in California will last for ages to come."

For immediate needs an act authorized the issuance of bonds to a maximum of $300,000, interest at three per cent a month, payable in six months. Governor Burnett signed the bill February 1, 1850.

To provide permanent revenue, the legislature taxed real and personal property at 50¢ per $100 of assessed value. The Californios opposed it vigorously as taxing their large land holdings heavily and unfairly. The American majority outvoted them.

The poll tax of $5 on every white male inhabitant between 21 and 50 years-old was aimed at miners in the prime of life.

Green authored the Foreign Miners' Tax Law that called for issuing licenses to foreigners for $20 a month. He itemized its results: An estimated $200,000 income each month, protection of aliens, and eviction of "unprotected aliens" (those who failed to pay). It would discourage immigration and "put Americans on equal footing with foreigners." Collectors would make a commission of $5 on each permit sold.

The Assembly passed it: 19-4. The enthusiastic Senate gave Green a special commendation for his "splendid plan" and passed it: 11-2.

The bigoted bill encouraged prejudice already rampant in the mines. It proved troublesome and brought in little revenue, $26,574.89 from July 1 to December 15, 1850. Tax collectors experienced difficulty in collection. An uprising occurred at Sonora when French and Mexican miners combined and called upon all foreigners "not to allow yourselves to be fleeced by a band of miserable wretches repudiated by their own country." A volunteer militia drove out many foreigners.

There were other difficulties. Swindlers, posing as collectors, extorted the fee. Foreigners with licenses were driven from the diggings by ruffians. Collector L. A. Besancon attempted redress: "Common justice demanding that they should be protected in their labor or money returned." Incidentally, he was fired by Burnett for not being in sympathy with the law.

The law, aimed mainly at Mexicans, Chileans, and Peruvians, would be repealed in 1851. A more moderate version surfaced later, aimed against the Chinese.

The legislature looked to gambling as another lucrative revenue source. By day and night, gambling engaged every class—preachers, judges, clerks, merchants, laborers, and miners. During the rainy winters, miners spent thousands in gold dust in gambling halls and saloons.

Members enacted a law licensing each table at $10. Saloon keepers paid willingly for the protection and legal sanction it gave their "gambling hells." The fee seemed minor compared to income. San Francisco's aristocratic Parker House paid rent of $60,000 a year for its attic, given over to gambling. Individual tables rented for $1,000 a month.

Creation of a framework for local government had priority. The Committee for Counties divided the state into twenty-seven counties and designated county seats. Mariano Vallejo, with his thorough knowledge of California, acted as Chairman for the derivation and definition of names of the original counties. With the exception of Sutter and Butte counties, all were of Spanish and Indian derivation. His report, containing many anecdotes, is still of historical interest.

Several laws pertained to the incorporation of cities and towns. Sonoma, Los Angeles, and Santa Barbara gained city status under a law providing for granting incorporation by legislature or county court. Benicia, San Diego, Monterey, San José, and San Francisco incorporated under a Special Act providing for particular places.

The creation of a code of laws, vital to the workings of the state, touching the lives of all people, could be classed as the legislature's major contribution. A series of acts abolished courts of the occupation and provided for a complete judicial system—courts, officers, districts, and procedures.

The Judiciary Committee formulated a code of laws encompassing criminal law, civil cases, social and business relations and numerous other concerns.

Governor Burnett recommended a combination of the best of civil law and the American system of common law. But the report of the Honorable Elisha O. Crosby, a lawyer of outstanding ability, had greater impact. He recalled later, "I never worked harder than in the winter of '49 and the spring of '50."

Crosby's report reviewed the history and contrasted the contributions of civil and common law. Its conclusions: Civil law with its strict controls looked to the spirit of the past, hampering progress. Common law emphasized the freedom and responsibility of man, promoting progress. Trial by jury and the writ of *Habeas Corpus*—valued highly by Americans—were unknown to civil law. The education and practice of American lawyers was based on common law.

In his inaugural speech, Governor Burnett had set a pattern for racism in California by advocating the exclusion of Negroes from the state. He reflected the bigotry characteristic of the legislature and the larger population at the time.

A law setting initial procedures for civil and criminal cases provided: "no black or mulatto person, or Indian shall be permitted to give evidence in any action to which a white person is a party in any court in this state." It remained on the books for thirteen years.

A bill to prevent the immigration of free Negroes passed in the Assembly. When it came up in the Senate, David C. Broderick, anti-slavery advocate, moved that it be indefinitely postponed and the motion carried.

The legislators had ample opportunities for amusement as well as work and took full advantage of them. In 1898, half-a-century later, the Honorable E. W. McKinstry in a speech at San José's Golden Jubilee stated: It is sad to remember that the work of the pioneer Legislature was accomplished amidst the distractions of monte, faro, and lasquenet;

of practical jokes, mostly of the sham duel order; of quarter races and bull-fights, billiard matches and fandangos.

Their rough and ready masculine manners and humor smacked more of the frontier than the parlor. A favorite joke provoked guffaws echoing throughout the chambers. On their way upstairs to attend night meetings, assemblymen carried candles to light their way. A revolver shot often snuffed out the flame, startling the victim and leaving him in darkness. Of course, the perpetrators had reputations as crack marksmen.

On Sunday, March 3rd, a titanic joke involved the entire community. A rumor circulated that gold had been discovered in the bed of Coyote Creek. Members of the legislature and clerks rushed for picks, shovels and pans determined to "strike it rich." The mania lasted for twenty-four hours with no gold to show for it. Many shame-faced members refused to confess they had responded to the rumor.

Nightlife consisted of frequent fandangos, common name for Mexican-inspired dances. At the public fandango halls, men kept their hats on and treated their partners after each dance—coffee for the señoritas; something stronger for the señores. The Spanish elite gave highly respected private parties. San José "society" entertained at quiet dinner parties.

The legislature viewed bull fights and bull and bear fights with ambivalence. Many disapproved of these bloody encounters, yet they continued to attend. A more humane member introduced a resolution to obtain the names of those who witnessed a bull and bear fight the previous Sunday. Members quickly "sat down" the suggestion by an 18 to 7 vote.

The Assembly on April 14, 1851 dispatched the Sergeant-at-Arms to round-up absentees. One writer has it that the majority of members had gone to witness the combat between a bull and bear.

The pleasure-loving Spanish delighted in festivals at any time, particularly on Sundays and important holidays. Bull fighting and bear-and-bull contests commonly took place on the plaza in front of St. Joseph's Church. Priests and congregation alike cheered on the contest between man and beast and beast and beast after mass.

The bull fighter entered the arena with a red blanket and knife. He flaunted the blanket before the enraged bull, springing aside at the last second. At each pass he endeavored to plant the knife in the vulnerable spot behind the horns. Excitement ran highest when the bull died or the man was thrown over the fence.

For a bull and bear fight you first needed a live grizzly. Three or four vaqueros on horses trained not to panic at the scent of the bear rode forth together. A

The bull and bear, chained together, fought until death, providing bloody entertainment for the first legislators.

Photo from California State Library

lasso thrown over the animal's head and quickly drawn taut choked him. Other lasso throws caught the bear's hind legs. Half strangled, pulled apart as horses backed up in opposite directions, the grizzly was made helpless in a matter of minutes. A third man dismounted and tied the feet together then wound the rope around and around. The enraged beast, trussed and helpless as a Thanksgiving turkey, was placed on a bullock hide drawn by horses, or in an oxen-drawn *carreta* bound for the arena.

The bear was chained to a post restricting the animal to a fifteen to twenty foot circle. The bull, on release from a darkened stall, had the freedom of the arena. The fury of the maddened bull, the brute strength of the one-thousand-pound bear, huge paws raised to parry his enemy, hushed the audience. The bear tried to grasp the bull's vulnerable tongue or nose. The bull gored the bear with his sharp curved horns. Usually the fight ended in a bloody draw with both animals near-dead or dead.

Horseraces and cockfights added to the carnival atmosphere on Sundays. Only when women came in

greater numbers was an ordinance enacted to prevent noisy and barbarous amusements on the Sabbath.

Now back to work with the problems that preoccupied the lawmakers. On January 29, 1850, their discontent erupted once again in a Senate bill directing the Building Commission to find a suitable location "at a point approachable by a large steamer and distant from any town." A naive belief existed that the legislators freed from temptation, in an atmosphere conducive to pure thought, would produce better laws.

The *pueblo* of San José offered its best to the lawmakers. Actually, they would have found much the same conditions in any California town. Why then were they so discontented?

Writers have suggested the *pueblo* was "too Mexican" and too isolated. In the wet winter of 1849-50, the stage discontinued services. The legislators were virtually marooned. Although only six miles from the Embarcadero, it had turned into a vast six-mile lake.

Citizens induced boarding house keepers and hotels to accept state scrip at par. Even this failed to soften the grumbling. Prominent men foresaw the capital and the prestige and prosperity that went with it slipping away.

James Reed and Charles White had lobbied for the capital at the Constitutional Convention. Now, they were the first to come forward with incentives to remain.

Reed offered four blocks of land for building sites, plus 168 lots to be sold at auction with proceeds to finance building costs. If the State preferred, he would give two lots for building sites and 200 lots to sell.

On the same day, January 30, 1850, White presented his offer for the legislature's approval: one and one-half square miles of land three miles from the *pueblo's* center, including a stream of pure water and building stone. Part would be used for public buildings, the rest sold with one-third to go to White and two-thirds to the state's building fund.

On February 4th, Dr. John Townsend and others offered 200 acres near town. The acreage could be used for state buildings (except for a penitentiary) and the balance sold.

Other cities made proposals. A letter from Monterey offered Colton Hall and 1,000 acres of land for botanical gardens, prison, or whatever the State wished.

New York of the Pacific, promoted by Colonel Jonathan D. Stevenson who envisioned a future city as great as his native New York, made an offer as pretentious as its name: free quarters furnished complete with desk and chairs "equal to those used in the Senate and House of Representatives of the United

States Congress in Washington" and a governor's mansion not to exceed $100,000.

Stevenson and W. C. Parker had formed a partnership, combining their resources to buy the 10,000-acre Rancho Los Medanos on the Carquinez Straits, sixty-five miles from San Francisco (present Pittsburg). Their dream city grew to three houses before dying of disappointment. No one voted for it as a capital.

Sacramento made its first bid for the capital, as did a number of other cities.

Don Mariano Guadalupe Vallejo's grandiose projected capital towered above all others. He presented a memorial setting forth his offer of 156 acres of land, of the State's choosing, on the Carquinez Straits and a donation of $370,000 for buildings. Plans for the made-to-order capital included a Capitol building, State offices, State library, university, schools, hospitals, orphanages, botanical gardens, and even a $3,000 mineral cabinet.

Vallejo promoted *Eureka* as the "truest centre" of the state for commerce, population, and travel. It fulfilled admirably the specific requirements of accessibility by steamboat and isolation.

Vallejo concluded:

> Shall it be said, then, while the whole world is coveting our possession of what all acknowledge to be the half-way house of the world's commerce, the great Bay of San Francisco, that the people of the rich possession are so unmindful of its value as not to honor her magnificent shores with a capital worthy of a great state?

His friends overruled his suggestion for a name. They called the city which would spring up where only wild oats and mustard flourished, Vallejo, in his honor.

The Senate Committee on Public Buildings and Grounds agreed that Vallejo was the "truest centre" and expressed enthusiasm for the project.

The Honorable David C. Broderick presented the majority opinion in a flowery accolade:

> Your committee cannot dwell with too much warmth upon the magnificent propositions contained in the memorial of General Vallejo. They breathe throughout the spirit of an enlarged mind, and a sincere public benefactor, for which he deserves the thanks of his countrymen and the admiration of the world. Such a proposition looks more like the legacy of a mighty Emperor to his people than the free donation of a private planter to a great State, yet poor in public finance, but soon to be among the first of the earth.

The committee argued that four-fifths of the state's future population, due to the mines, would live near the Sacramento, San Joaquin, and Trinity Rivers. Furthermore, since the state had no money in the treasury, it was good sense, indeed necessary to accept Vallejo's generous offer.

San José offered land. Vallejo topped the offer with a capital city of magnificent proportions, free to the state.

Many felt it advisable to obtain the opinion of the people. On April 22, 1850, a bill passed "to take the Sense of the People of the State of California upon the Subject of Permanent location of the Seat of Government." All propositions were to be voted on by October 7, 1850.

The legislature adjourned with the vital question still unanswered. Where was the capital to be?

Before the close of the session on April 22, Governor Burnett had found it impossible to keep up with the paperwork, so fast did bills cross his desk. He channeled some to the Secretary of State, William Van Voorhies, and some to his private secretary. After a single reading, on their recommendation, Burnett signed his name. Unapologetic, he wrote, "I had to do this or let the government go on with a mutilated code of statutory law, or call an extra session."

The pioneer legislature had passed 146 acts signed by the Governor and 19 joint resolutions, having been in session a little over four months. In Governor Burnett's estimation:

> The first session of our legislature was one of the best we have ever had. The members were honest, indefatigable workers. The long-continued rainy season and the want of facilities for dispatching business were great obstacles in their way. Besides, they had to begin at the beginning and create an entirely new code of statute law, with but few authorities to consult. Under the circumstances, their labors were most creditable.

Senator Thomas Jefferson Green and journalists who found it impossible to reject a catchy phrase are chiefly responsible for the label "The Legislature of a Thousand Drinks." Green kept a supply of liquor nearby for lobbying purposes and gathered a coterie of hangers-on who "cut up their pranks." On the day's adjournment he invariably invited, "Well, boys let's take a thousand drinks."

John Bidwell, later candidate for Presidency of the United States on the Prohibition ticket, and General Vallejo, who seldom sipped even his own prize-winning wines, served the same legislature. David C. Broderick seldom drank—his vice was ambition. Dr. Benjamin Cory, the first physician in Santa Clara County, Judge McKinstry, Elisha Crosby—all were men of temperate habits.

The excitement of "gold fever" that permeated the air, the dominant young male society, the saloon's function as social and business center encouraged drinking. Yet, few legislators were habitual drinkers.

Historian Theodore Hittell reiterated:

> It is certain that no legislature has ever sat in the State that did more work, more important work, or better work. If anything is to be said about the drinking of such a body, it ought to be something similar to the answer attributed to Lincoln about Grant. When complaint was made that Grant drank too much whiskey, Lincoln replied that he would like to get the brand of that whiskey to give to his other generals.

Bancroft says succinctly, "It was the best legislature California ever had. All were honest—there was nothing to steal."

Although the first session of the legislature had adjourned, Californians still waited impatiently for official sanction. California's delegates to Congress camped on the stairs of the Capitol awaiting admission.

Admission of California threatened the carefully maintained balance between free and slave states, the institution of slavery, and the Union itself.

After heated debate and compromise, the bill admitting California to the Union finally passed Congress in August and was signed by President Fillmore, September 9, 1850.

On October 18, the steamer *Oregon* sailed into San Francisco's harbor swathed with bunting and flags from bow to stern. Banners proclaimed "California is a state." Gun after gun fired, the echoes resounding in a salute to the Thirty-first State. Men leaped from the decks shouting the news. Every ship in the harbor raised the stars and stripes. At Portsmouth Square zealous hands hoisted the flag, its 31st star cut from paper.

San Francisco exploded in a spontaneous spree. Merchants ran to the docks, forgetting their hats, leaving their businesses unattended. Bells rang from churches and firehouses. Dancing and music from a hundred bands filled the streets. Saloons ran low on champagne as celebrators toasted: "To California and the Union," "To Thomas Benton," "To California's great future," etc. That evening candles illuminated windows. Bonfires blazed on the hills. Skyrockets spangled the air.

That night Governor Burnett took part in the enthusiastic meeting at Portsmouth Square where $5,000 was raised for a formal celebration with processions, orations, and a grand ball on October 29th.

The next morning the Governor left for San José on Hall and Crandall's stage coach line. Jared B. Crandall, a stage whip of the first caliber, drove with Burnett on the seat beside him. Together with a rival Concord coach they raced to San José fifty miles away. Crandall lashed the six mustangs; "away they whirled through the oak openings and across the plains." Burnett described it, "As we flew past on our rapid course, the people flocked to the road to see what caused our rapid driving and loud shouting. Without slackening our speed in the slightest degree, we took off our hats, waved them around our heads, and shouted at the tops' of our voices, "California is admitted into the Union!"...I never witnessed a scene more exciting, and never felt more enthusiastic."

The ride insured Crandall's fame. His rival finished five minutes later. No one mentions his name.

Along with the enthusiasm, cheers, and gaiety a feeling of piety prevailed. The Honorable Elisha McKinstry remembered, "...thousands of grateful hearts were bowed in pious thankfulness that at last California was recognized as an equal and integral part of our glorious land."

Messengers circulated the good news throughout California. A Sacramento steamer shrieked the tidings with its whistle at river landings. At last California had "political as well as personal ties" to the States.

The second general election under the constitution, with voting on legislators, state officers, and capital proposals took place October 7th. Vallejo won by a wide margin with 7,477 votes. San José came in a poor second with 1,292 votes and 651 for James Reed's proposition. Monterey with 399 votes was third.

At the time, Don Mariano Guadalupe Vallejo was considered the wealthiest man in the entire state. He owned 146,000 acres, including the 80,000-acre Rancho Soscol on the shores of Suisun Bay, site of Vallejo. True he suffered losses of $100,000 in destroyed buildings, stock, and crops in the Bear Flag Rebellion. But, the high prices of the gold rush greatly increased the value of his cattle, horses, and grain crops.

Only a few men voiced doubts as to Vallejo's ability to conjure up a capital city.

John McDougal, second governor of California.

CHAPTER VI
Still in San José
Second Session: 1851

When the legislature opened for its second session January 6, 1851, it remained in San José, but with a difference—California assumed status as the thirty-first state.

Governor Burnett presented his annual message the next day. Burnett's views hadn't changed. He liked to think of himself as unprejudiced, and therefore went into long explanations of reasons for his prejudices. He stated: "That a war of extermination will continue to be waged between the races, until the Indian race becomes extinguished must be expected." In most instances, he had left people of each region to protect themselves against attack "except where two immigrant trails enter the state."

Burnett repeated his belief that "free persons of color" should be excluded from the state. He suggested the death penalty for grand larceny and robbery. Only in this way could the "frightful increase in crime" be dealt with and citizens prevented from taking justice into their hands. He admitted this would be changed when prisons became available.

The Governor also recommended reduction in state salaries. "High salaries excite more the cupidity of men than their patriotism."

By December 15, 1850, the government that started out penniless owed $485,460.28. Burnett had refused to call an extra session to procure another loan. He advised, "...make *more*, spend *less*, and borrow *none*." He had no thoughts on how to implement his advice. The only means of obtaining money seemed to be bonds to be sold in the east where interest rates were lower.

Burnett reiterated the difficulties of establishing and administering a new government adapted to California's particular circumstances: "Our people formed a mixed and multitudinous host; from almost every clime and nation in the world, with all their discordant views, feelings, and opinions."

Surprising everyone, on January 9th Governor Burnett tendered his resignation to devote full attention to private affairs. Senator Elisha Crosby, although paying tribute to Burnett's honesty and good intentions, characterized him as lacking "backbone" under the multitude of pressures requiring decisive action.

The legislature accepted Burnett's resignation in the morning and inaugurated Lieutenant Governor McDougal in the afternoon.

McDougal had been elected Lieutenant Governor in a landslide even though he ran against men with far more ability. A jovial extrovert, he made friends easily. Chameleonlike, he adapted his opinions readily so made few enemies. People voted for him without thought, simply because they liked him. They considered a Lieutenant Governor just about as important as fool's gold.

His tolerant contemporaries described McDougal as a "gentlemanly drunkard." His "freaks of behavior" and continual over-indulgence indicate he was already a full-blown alcoholic. A colleague said,

"McDougal largely destroyed his usefulness at the Constitutional Convention by drinking too much." The same could be said of his term as governor.

When Governor McDougal took the oath of office, he addressed the legislature briefly, stating distrust of his abilities and giving assurance of cooperation. With the elevation to governor, he assumed an authoritative air. He dressed like a nabob in old style ruffled shirt, buff vest and pantaloons, and blue coat with brass buttons. His pompous manner together with his style in issuing proclamations earned him the nickname of "I, John."

Controversy over the removal of the capital became a bitterly fought annual ritual. Soon after the legislature opened, Martin E. Cooke, Senator from Solano, presented Vallejo's statement that he was prepared to enter into ample bonds, insuring the donation of $370,000 for capital buildings.

The next day, Cooke procured approval for the Surveyor-General to report on the peculiarities and advantages of all proposed capital sites. Ten days later Charles Whiting presented a short unsatisfactory report: Vallejo's chief advantage lay in accessibility, on the direct route to the mining districts; easily reached by steamer from other points. The same might be said of New York of the Pacific. As to San José, communication during the rainy season was most unpleasant "to say the least of it," although construction of a railroad would eliminate the difficulty.

Cooke next introduced a bill for permanent location of the capital at Vallejo along with the report from the Committee on Building. He pointed out Vallejo's advantages adding some new ones: Nine-tenths of the state officials passed Vallejo on the way to San José, so the state would save thousands on mileage paid out. "There are no diseases incident to the place," since it has abundant good water and excellent climate. Lumber and building materials could be easily transported by ship for state buildings. Finally, in case of war the town could be easily defended. The question should be settled immediately, he urged "to put the public mind to rest" and take steps for the erection of state buildings.

Minority leader, George Tingley fought mightily against removal. He pronounced Vallejo's project as "handsome arrayed in tall columns of figures" and "filled to overflowing with gold...in reality, a speculative project to enrich individuals." To remove the Seat of Government, he argued, would require large expenditures. "States, like individuals, had better pay their debts before contracting for the erection of splendid edifices..."

Tingley restated San José advantages: A beautiful valley, a climate equal to Italy's and comfortable buildings furnished free to the state.

He asked: "If Vallejo possessed such peculiar advantages for a large commercial city, why have not the *keen* eyes of California *city builders* long since detected it?" He contended that although 8,000 to 10,000 voted for Vallejo out of 100,000 population, most voted for the name of Vallejo or to accommodate a friend. Sarcastically, he pointed out, "There could hardly be disease there since there was not a living resident or buildings." Tingley reminded that Vallejo had not yet deeded the proposed acreage worth about $5 an acre to the state nor was it known for sure that the title was good.

Once again Elisha Crosby presented San José's counter offer of suitable state offices free of charge until the state decided to build—if only the legislature would remain. His entreaties failed to impress anyone.

The Vallejo bill and an amendment providing that failure of any part would void the whole passed the Senate. The vote: eleven ayes - two noes (Crosby and Tingley). The bill for removal was rushed through the Assembly and received the Governor's approval February 4, 1851.

Vallejo's bond for $500,000 with attached affidavits listed Vallejo's assets at one million, John Frisbie's at $75,000, Salvador Vallejo's at $250,000, Robert Allen's at $100,000, and James Estell's at $60,000.

As might be expected Tingley protested: "Men of *hundreds of thousands of today*, are assignees and bankrupts of tomorrow, in California." He recommended mortgages on real property as security with a cash value of at least $500,000.

While Tingley objected, Vallejo deeded over an indefinite number of acres for the projected capital city, the land to be selected by five commissioners.

After diligent examination of the land and the selection of building sites, the Commissioners reported back (March 25th). The projected plans, if only carried out, would have made the capital a "future city" envied and copied worldwide.

The committee selected a hill overlooking Napa Bay for the Capitol, Governor's mansion, and university. On a clear day the 360 degree view encompassed the city of San Francisco, and the fertile valleys of Napa, Sonoma, Petaluma, San Pablo, and San Rafael. Mt. Diablo peak dominated the landscape.

The site for the university looked down on the Capitol. The commissioners wondered: "Would a more secluded site be best?" They decided, "...youth, during his collegiate course, would gain more information from Legislative debates, than from the ablest professorship."

The valley selected for the Lunatic Asylum had "advantages of the stir from the great highway or rural quiet, as the medical facility may prescribe." Each of the sites for the Deaf and Dumb Asylum,

Asylum for the Blind, and Orphan Asylum had distinct advantages. Commissioners assigned the male and female hospitals a place near natural hot tubs of curative mineral springs. Four two-acre plots at convenient points were set aside for schools.

A prominent hill on the Carquinez Straits seemed the best site for a penitentiary for several reasons: proximity to the bay made transport easy. Also, "…its formidable walls, immediately on the great highway to our inexhaustible gold mines, will stand as warning to the shiploads of rascals congregating hither from the penal colonies of other nations."

At last, it seemed California had found a permanent capital and the indecision and wrangling would be put to rest. Instead charges of bribery proliferated. San José had counted noses daily and up to the hour of final vote, more-than-enough promises assured the capital would remain. Citizens suspected Vallejo had passed out deeds to lots freely in exchange for votes. On April 11th, Isaac N. Thorne requested a committee of investigation. It was duly appointed by the legislature only to be dissolved the next day. Historian Hittell suggests an investigation would have disclosed "facts of a startling nature."

The disgruntled merchants and boarding-house keepers of San José no longer felt obliged to take scrip at par value. They informed the legislators politely that from now on they would accept payment in gold.

Despite preoccupation with the capital, the legislature of 1851 could point to worthwhile accomplishments.

Competent Stephen Field, later Judge of the United States Supreme Court, served on the Judiciary Committee and reviewed the codes of civil and criminal procedure of New York. He then remodeled them to fit California conditions based on the latest legal reforms. The Civil Practice Act and Criminal Practice Act served as models for all other states west of the Rocky Mountains.

Field stated, "I recast in two acts over three hundred sections and added over one hundred new ones."

Statues of special importance incorporated in the code included provisions regarding the forced sale of personal property, Homestead Exemption Act, and the divorce act.

About the provision exempting personal property of the debtor, Stephen J. Field remarked, "I never could appreciate the wisdom of stripping a poor debtor of all needed articles of his household and of implements by which…he could earn the means of …ultimately discharging his obligations."

The important Homestead Act exempted homestead and other property amounting to $5,000. It had been advocated by Burnett but failed to pass the assembly in 1850.

The Assembly passed the divorce bill after stiff debate by one vote (18-17). In the Senate, Elcan Heydenfeldt presented the majority report against divorce. The report conceded that courts could grant divorce for "insuperable" causes existing before marriage, such as impotence. Otherwise, marriage, a religious sacrament, should never be dissolved except by death.

Tingley's minority opinion termed the reasoning "illogical." In impassioned words he set forth the circumstances under which marriage becomes a "distressing burden to both parties and a festering curse upon the community."

To augment his case against divorce, Heydenfeldt presented petitions signed by residents of San José, Mission San José, and San Francisco. When the petitions netted little results, he invited a Baptist preacher to deliver a sermon against divorce. The outraged Senate, quickly censured Heydenfeldt for misuse of his powers.

Bitterly contested, the divorce bill finally passed the Senate and received the Governor's signature.

The act granting tidal water lots to the city of San Francisco (known as the Water Lot Bill) opened up charges of bribery and corruption. Introduced February 1851, it went through a series of reconsiderations and amendments before becoming a law on March 26th. An investigation committee was formed only to be dissolved. Serious charges that lawmakers had accepted bribes continued, renewing investigation. The committee submitted testimony of an incriminating nature, but before the most important witnesses appeared, the legislature adjourned. On the motion of John Bigler, the testimony was erased from the *Journal* and filed in the office of the Secretary of State, effectively closing the case.

Bribery was elevated to a fine art during the first years of California politics. Bancroft explained:

> A kind of moral intoxication, a gold-drunkenness, had debased the public mind and distorted the spiritual vision, until men esteemed it a distinction to become noted for procuring or handling, even for stealing, large sums of money; and it was only when their own fortunes, or their lives, were in danger, that their fellows plucked up courage to rebuke them.

The case of Senator Alonzo W. Adams, former collector of foreign miner's licenses, was also buried. Adams exposed extravagance in the State Printing Department. Revenging parties in turn attacked the Senator. Some accounts leave the impression that Adams diverted large sums of public revenue to himself. Others, that he fully settled accounts by returning unsold licenses. In any event, a committee examined his papers, but before their report Adams resigned and took a steamer, destination unknown. The papers were sealed and filed in the office of the Secretary of State.

Meeting jointly the legislature turned its attention to the election of a United States Senator on February 10th. Fremont had abandoned his senate duties, returning home early to campaign for reelection. He received eight votes on the first ballot, twenty-five being necessary. Fremont's exploits in the Bear Flag episode and Conquest already seemed long ago. The convention balloted 142 times over a period of ten days with no winner. For awhile, Senator Gwin held sway in the United States Senate alone.

McDougal's tenure saw the establishment of a State Marine Hospital in San Francisco. Hospitals at Stockton and Sacramento provided care for the sick and mentally ill patients in the mining areas.

Indian wars presented problems for the governors. Although the state militia protected the citizens, no provision was made for paying them. McDougal called the need to the legislature's attention and they enacted a measure providing for compensation for militia duty.

David C. Broderick, President of the Senate, and John Bigler, Speaker of the Assembly, spoke briefly before adjournment on May 1, 1851. Bigler remarked on the important accomplishments of the Assembly. The session had been longer than expected, but many vital questions had been determined: 120 bills had been passed and approved by the governor.

Broderick and Bigler would form a political partnership with far-reaching consequences for California.

Foolishly, Governor McDougal ordered the state offices and archives removed to Vallejo without prior approval of the legislature (June 1851). By September he realized progress proceeded at a snail's pace. The Governor declared the unfinished buildings unsafe for storage of the archives and requested return to San José.

A deluge of disapproval hailed from all quarters. In vehement print the newspaper, *Alta California* opined: "The state capital is being taken away from civilization to be located among the coyotes."

Lawyers gave their version of the Removal Bill: It was a contract, subject to various interpretations—not a law. Failure of fulfillment within three years voided the contract, but no timetable of completion was specified.

Alta California now took the position that the legislature should meet at Vallejo to avoid more expense. Moreover, General Vallejo and his partners would be in a position to sue the state, if the legislature failed to fulfill its obligations.

Alta California for October 14, 1851 continued its campaign:

> This paper opposed from the beginning the wild and speculating project of building a city where none existed, none was needed....But it had the assistance of no other press in the State, and the princely proposition, as it was called, seemed a pill so sweet, gilded as it was with a yellow promise of $370,000 cash on the nail, that the people swallowed it...It will take something more than prickly ash tea to heal the disorganization of the political system which has already grown, and is yet likely to grow out of this unfortunate movement.

On Christmas day 1851, the Superintendent of Public Buildings reported to Governor McDougal: "While the State House was better than San Jose's, other buildings were few, and lodgings decidedly inferior." Finally a meeting to decide on removal or alternatives took place in San Francisco in the District Court Room of the California Exchange (December 30th). Twelve senators and thirty assemblymen attended.

John Parrish of Yolo County favored meeting at Vallejo, the legal seat of government, the first Monday in January as planned.

George Tingley, still opposed removal, "Since the General had not fulfilled his contract, the law should be declared void."

Attorney-General James McDougall gave his legal opinion. General Vallejo had submitted a bond for approval. The provisions that Vallejo provide buildings within three years and that failure to do so voided the contract applied only after the legislature met at Vallejo in 1852. Failure to comply with part of the contract did not make all of it void. Also there was no stipulation as to a particular time.

Spirited debate followed the reading of the report of the Superintendent of Public Buildings. The resolution to open the session at the legal seat of government—Vallejo—won out, 28-13.

San José's growth slowed to a stall; business hovered in the doldrums. Angry citizens felt cheated at removal of the capital from the best location for the State's welfare—and their own.

CHAPTER VII

Vallejo's Unfinished Capitol

Third Session: 1852

All night Vallejo's carpenters worked in a furious flurry of activity to finish the State House before the legislators arrived.

Actually, General Vallejo had made a valiant try to fulfill his magnificent promises. The gold rush made labor and materials expensive and hard to come by. His uncooperative partners had shunted full responsibility to Vallejo's shoulders.

The legislators arrived, ill-humored, and muddy on January 5th. The boat from San Francisco grounded fifty feet from the wharf and passengers had to be rowed ashore. They trudged through streets filled with oceans of tar-like mud to the stark frame building on Capitol hill. They found the Assembly chamber on the lower floor and the Senate on the upper floor bare.

Seating had to be improvised from nail kegs or benches made by laying boards on stools—an uncomfortable arrangement, inclined to break without warning. There were no rostrums, no committee rooms, no printing facilities.

A saloon and a bowling alley, christened the "third House," occupied the basement, small consolation for the woeful inadequacies.

Primitive lodgings drew wrathful complaints. Price for the few available accommodations averaged $20 to $30 a week. The steamer "Empire," converted to a hotel, filled the gap, accommodating one hundred people. "Food was amusingly scarce," according to the *California Blue Book*, 1907. Just who was amused

is left in doubt. While the legislature convened on the sixth, the steamer journeyed to San Francisco to pick up more provisions.

An article in *Alta California* (January 8th) confirmed the "villianous accommodations." Evidently a fan of Mark Twain, the correspondent's exaggerated story told of three members who, having no other place to sleep, sat in chairs until nearly frozen numb. Then they ran around to warm up and repeated the process until morning.

Journalists devoted their full attention to conditions and complaints. On January 8th, they were finally able to report that enough chairs had arrived to replace the improvised benches.

Immediately after members took the oath of office, George Tingley and Frank Soulé presented a written protest. They declared the contract void since Vallejo had not provided adequate buildings. Further, convening the legislature would make Vallejo a legal capital. Their resolution was tabled.

Just before John Bigler's inauguration, Governor McDougal sent a protest to the Senate to the effect that since Vallejo failed to supply suitable buildings, the legislature should return to the legal seat of government—San José.

After being sworn into office, Governor Bigler delivered his inaugural address to both houses (January 9th). He stated his belief that the fewer and plainer the laws by which a people are governed the better. The Governor advocated a liberal policy

The bleak white statehouse at Vallejo, second capitol of California.

toward those who settled on "wilderness and tamed it into well-cultivated farms." Mines should be left free. He concluded with remarks on the slavery question and the hope that California would approve compromise measures and uphold the Union.

Bigler, also, injected some remarks about the times:

> The spirit of the age may truly be said to be the passion for wealth and luxury....When a people become so far enamored of gold as to gloss Guilt, and veil Ignorance when clothed in garb of wealth, then it is that virtue and real wealth began to totter, the reins of power gradually lapse into the hands of the inefficient and dishonest.

David C. Broderick had been influential in the nomination of Bigler for Governor in the first Democratic Convention in California (May 1851). He won over Pearson B. Reading by 370 undisputed votes and 70 disputed votes in a contested election. Contested elections became a pattern for Bigler. In the first state election, returns showed his opponent the winner; Bigler contested the election and won by fifty votes.

Governor Bigler and his family had come to California in 1849 and settled in Sacramento. Although he had studied law, at first he worked at odd jobs. He unloaded steamboats at Sacramento docks, cried wares at auctions, and stuffed comforters, receiving part of his pay in calico for dresses for his wife and daughter.

Bigler had endeared himself to Sacramento citizens in the cholera epidemic of 1850. Frightened people fled Sacramento by thousands. The death toll numbered at least five hundred, sixteen of them doctors. Without regard for his health, Bigler nursed those suffering from the disease. He contracted cholera and almost died.

Forty-seven years of age, short and rotund, Bigler was careless in manners and dress. His high hat perched precariously on the back of his head. He looked to the ordinary man—the squatters and miners—for political support. Energetic and quick to seize opportunity, he practiced politics with considerable success.

Corruption and furor marked Bigler's two terms. The furor over Vallejo was the first of many.

Ambitious cities saw opportunity. San Francisco offered any buildings the state might need. San José offered board at the bargain rate of $14 a week.

Benicia suggested her Masonic Hall for the Senate, the Presbyterian Church for the Assembly and a private residence for state offices.

Sacramento offered her two-story courthouse of generous dimensions, 50 feet by 70 feet, completed only two weeks before, and free tickets to the American Theatre.

Estell, a co-signer of Vallejo's performance bond, presented the petition from thirty-one beleagured citizens of Vallejo, pleading for more time and offering to supply suitable accommodations within one week. When this resolution lost, Estell proposed that the legislature recess for ten days.

On January 9th, 1852 the question opened for discussion in the Assembly. Dr. Austin Wing (El Dorado) submitted: "Resolved, the Senate concurring, that the legislature do adjourn for the time being to assemble on _____ day at the city of _____." The blanks to be filled in later. In a whirlwind of debate, Sacramento won, 30-26.

Sacramento had less strength in the Senate. After several alternatives were defeated, members voted on the Assembly bill with a tie vote. The tie was broken when Lieutenant Governor Purdy cast an adverse vote.

On January 12th, the bill was brought forward again. This time it passed. The legislature had suffered the uncomfortable capital for seven days. Monterey, Benicia, San José were suggested and rejected. David Broderick moved for Sacramento with a removal date the same as that of the Assembly bill, January 16th.

The population of Vallejo, which had counted on serving the legislators, held an indignation meeting. The delighted Assembly celebrated with an impromptu party at Wyatt House Bar. The Senate evidently remained dignified.

Sacramento lobbyists chartered the steamer *Empire* to take the legislators the 110 miles upriver. The captain refused to leave until paid his money, $1,700, in advance. Money paid, removal began. The *Alta California* for January 16, 1852 carried the story:

> Bright and early...the whole town was in commotion. Carpets were torn up from the floors, stoves and long stove pipes came down on the run, the China chairs were tumbled in a heap out of the State House and carried in homogeneous masses on men's heads down to the wharf. The barkeepers, finding their occupation was gone, concluded to stick by the Legislature as their only safeguard, and decanters and tumblers, bars and bar fixtures, stoughton bitters, silver-twirlers and champagne basket went pell-mell into confusion and down aboard the boat, mixed in with the legislators, judges, and private gentlemen who

Portrait of John Bigler, third governor of California.

Photo from the California State Library

merely came to see what the two Houses were doing. The barber put his razor, his indiscriminate hairbrush and supply of one towel into his pocket, shouldered his chair, and marched down to the *Empire* also.

In the midst of the confusion and general happiness, there was sadness: "Here and there only was a long face marking some speculator, who was standing bewildered in the turmoil, and saying to himself, "Fallen is Vallejo—Vallejo the magnificent!"

The *Empire* reached Sacramento the next day. They were received with music, oratory, cannon thunder, a parade and all the panoply the town could muster.

The citizens charged themselves $20 each for tickets to a grand ball at the Orleans Hotel. They invited one hundred ladies to entertain and dance with the legislators. For once there was no complaints. Both Houses concurred: they were delighted with the lavish hospitality, public buildings, and even accommodations.

The two-story Court House accommodated the Assembly in a room 34 feet by 80 feet on the second floor. The Senate met on the lower floor which also had two committee rooms, four offices and a fireproof vault.

Prominent citizen, Don Mariano Vallejo, was also an ardent family man. (He had sixteen children and adopted eight more.)   Photo from the California State Library

Although the legislators were comfortable at last, they definitely understood Sacramento was merely temporary. Vallejo still cherished hopes of completing his dream capital city.

When the Governor sent for the archives, he discovered they were still in San José. J. D. Hoppe had issued a restraining order and was holding them in the "true legal capital." Hoppe and other realtors, interested as financiers and patriotic citizens, began litigation over the legality of the capital. They used the argument that the Removal Act of 1851 was conditional on Vallejo fulfilling his contract. If the legislature wanted to change its capital, its action must be done at the legal capital. The matter was dissolved upon court hearing, records were removed and Sacramento became the temporary home of legislative and executive departments.

Vallejo's citizens submitted a list of items for which they demanded compensation. It was referred to a select committee. Members declined sympathy, "Citizens bent on speculation took their chances."

The legislature, anxious to know the status of the contract, appointed a committee of six to meet with Vallejo. Martin Cooke presented Vallejo's reply to the legislature on January 27, 1852:

"Sacramento
"January 24, 1852

"Gentlemen:
"I have to request that the Bond submitted by me in conformity with an Act passed February 14, 1851, 'providing for the permanent seat of Government of the State of California' be cancelled and annulled.

Many difficulties interposed at an early day after the passage of the act aforesaid, to embarrass me in the execution of the obligation imposed upon me by the provisions of that act. An association was formed by me with some of the most enterprising citizens of the State, with whose aid I proposed to develop the resources dedicated by me for the fulfillment of the obligations referred. This association, after much fruitless effort, gradually ceased to have any practical life or vigor, and I proceeded myself to provide a temporary State House and offices of the State....The credit and resources dedicated by me...have been shattered and destroyed.

"Very respectfully,
"M. G. Vallejo"

Clearly, M. G. Vallejo acknowledged failure of his grandiose gesture and wanted out of his contract. The legislature, comfortable in Sacramento, ignored the matter for the time being and turned their attention to other subjects.

Perhaps, at that point, the capital intended to remain at Sacramento.

On Sunday, March 7th, all Sacramento was awakened at 1 a.m. by the clanging of alarm bells—the levee on the American River had broken. Citizens rushed to fill the breach with timbers, sacks of barley, dirt, anything—but nothing could hold back the deluge. Two bridges snapped, cutting off communication. With temporary embankments swept away, flood waters submerged most of the city by evening. Crowds of people, animals, and tents congregated on higher lands near the plaza.

Legislators commuted to the courthouse by boat. Senator Paul Hubbs was absent, marooned at home.

Despite inconvenience, the waterlogged lawmakers retained their sense of humor. Charles Lott of Butte offered a resolution that the Committee on Commerce and Navigation procure boats and sailors to carry members to and from the Capitol. Tingley moved that the resolution be referred to the Committee on Swamp Lands, but Mr. Lott understood this Committee was swamped. Royal Sprague of Shasta suggested having the Committee find which streams within city lands were navigable.

Thomas Van Buren of San Joaquin wondered if the legislature had been duped—this was not the first time Sacramento had been inundated. Sacramento

Mariano Guadalupe Vallejo.
Photo from the California Department of Parks and Recreation

had experienced floods in 1850 and would again until the streets were raised.

The familiar agitation for removal resounded in the legislative chambers. Members talked of meeting in San Francisco, but finally decided to "stick it out."

During March and April a deluge of offers flooded the legislature as city bid against city. On March 16th Sacramento boldly renewed its offer of the Court House. The City of Monterey offered public buildings. On the 18th Benicia's offer of the City Hall was referred to the Committee on Public Buildings.

On March 31st, state officers authorized return to Vallejo at the end of the session.

Citizens of Martinez rushed in with an offer of public buildings, referred to the standing committee.

An "Act for the permanent location of the Seat of Government," declaring Vallejo the legal seat, passed the Assembly 29-20 on April 8th and on the 14th passed the Senate, 14-9.

The Act spurred Sacramento to greater efforts. To its former proposal, the Common Council added the public square on Ninth and Tenth Streets.

Sacramento had been a temporary expediency. The removal act for the transfer to Sacramento was declared void after May 4th. The Treasury appropriated $1,200 for moving the archives and state officers back to Vallejo in June. Vallejo would have a second chance.

The legislature somehow managed to sandwich solid work in between consideration of the capital and the flood. After 104 ballots, the legislators had given up on their attempt to elect a U. S. Senator in 1851. This time, David Broderick, running for Senator for the first time, was defeated by John Weller. Broderick persisted in his unswerving fight for political power, finally becoming a U. S. Senator in 1857.

The bill authorizing married women to transact business as sole traders was hailed as exceedingly liberal at the time.

Not so enlightened were bills directed against Blacks, Chinese, and Indians. A fugitive slave bill passed the Senate requiring return of runaway slaves to their masters. Although the Constitution prohibited slavery, it was not regarded as a legislative enactment. It became a law on Bigler's signature April 15, 1852. Hittell states: "It was not better or worse than fugitive slave laws of other states."

Anti-Chinese feeling also accelerated. At first, the Chinese had been treated with consideration. Few in number, they performed jobs scorned by Americans. But as the meek, cheap "coolie" (as they were called) competed with miners, anger erupted.

Chinese in California numbered about 27,000 in 1851. Quiet, industrious, and peaceful in manner, the Chinese kept together and kept their "curious" customs in food and dress intact.

The Chinese submitted to ill treatment patiently, worked mines abandoned by others, and paid the foreign miner's license of $3 a month. The fact that there was no real substance for their prejudices further aggravated the miners' anger. Right or wrong the "coolie" was clearly inferior and therefore, should be relegated to inferior jobs.

Nearly all Chinese emigrants came to California under a contract system with passage paid. In return they guaranteed to work for a certain time at a certain wage, their affairs handled by Chinese associations. Tingley introduced a bill for enforcing such contracts. It was killed by objections that such a bill would effectively degrade labor and increase ruinous competition. China would empty its prisons of every criminal. "Our own people would be exposed to foul leprosy and plague."

Governor Bigler, playing to the miners' vote, intensified anti-Chinese sentiment in a blatantly bigoted message stressing the importance of checking Chinese emigration. He advocated use of tax power and demanded that Congress prohibit "coolies" from labor in the mines.

Rather than enhancing Bigler's popularity, reaction condemned the Governor for encouraging outrages against the Chinese.

Bigler also echoed the feelings of Governor Burnett and many Californians regarding the "war of extermination" against Indians. The current policy called for removing Indians to isolated areas. Bigler felt the best policy would be the removal of all Indians from the state. In his opinion, it was the obligation of the federal government to finance expeditions against Indian tribes.

The Governor's policy in sending out relief expeditions came under much adverse criticism. An Act passed to aid overland emigrants, caught in the snows of the Sierra Nevada, authorized Bigler to determine relief measures with expenditures not to exceed $25,000. He appointed three senators as agents and sent out heavily-laden pack trains in June, before the emigrants arrival. Posts were established at Humboldt Sink, Truckee, and Carson River. Expenditures amounted to $32,500, an overrun of $7,500.

Outspoken Edward Gilbert, editor-in-chief for *Alta California*, charged Bigler with diverting funds for personal gain. State Senator James Denver, a friend of Bigler's who had acted as one of the agents, demanded a retraction and lambasted Gilbert's character.

Incensed, Gilbert replied to Denver with a duelling challenge. They fought at sunrise using Wesson rifles. The first volley missed. At the second, Gilbert fell mortally wounded. Popular, elegant, thirty-two-year-old Gilbert had served with distinction at the Constitutional Convention and as a representative to Congress. Gloom settled over San Francisco.

Bigler rewarded Denver by appointing him Secretary of State in 1853.

Marred as it was by corruption, Bigler's administration has been evaluated as among the poorest in the nineteenth century. Yet he was to be elected for a second term.

By now, the public had become thoroughly puzzled as to whether the "floating capital" would be found in San José, Vallejo, Sacramento, or _____.

CHAPTER VIII
Vallejo's Failure—Benicia's Brief Glory
Fourth Session: 1853

Vallejo had a second chance when the fourth session of the legislature convened there on January 3, 1853. A few iron buildings had been imported from Hawaii for use as state offices. Vallejo's dream capital remained a magnificent mirage.

For their convenience, a wagon drawn by mules awaited to carry legislators and their baggage through muddy streets. The coyote's serenade still filled the night air, heightening the sense of loneliness and desolation.

At least chairs and desks furnished the chambers and committee rooms of the bleak white State House.

The question of the capital loomed uppermost in everyone's mind. The Governor's annual message distracted the attention of the legislators for awhile.

Bigler's annual message to both houses concentrated on his concern with escalating budget deficits. He pointed out ways to curtail expenditures by strict policies of reduction in government: a biennial legislature, elimination of the superintendent of instruction, and decreasing judicial districts. He recommended reducing state salaries and payment in cash rather than scrip valued at one-third less than face value.

At the same time, he made suggestions for increased revenues. The most important: The water front of San Francisco should be extended and leased for state revenue, estates without legal heirs should revert to the state, and taxes should be enforced against steamships.

True to his role as "Father of the squatter" Bigler believed the legislature should demand that Congress free public lands for settlers. Also, he recommended early reclamation of swamp lands to be given to settlers in amounts not to exceed 320 acres.

The 1852 legislature had passed an act to procure a state prison and selected twenty acres of ground at San Quentin. The Governor stated the law was defective and needed revision. He spoke of his belief in the desirability of a Pacific Railroad. He omitted mention of Vallejo's inadequacies.

The see-saw of proposals and decisions began in earnest on January 7th. The Assembly's resolution that both houses meet with M. G. Vallejo was tabled. On January 12th, the Senate agreed on Vallejo as a capital city, and felt that roving about destroyed credibility and confidence in state government.

Dissatisfaction with conditions multiplied. The Senate reversed its decision and requested the Governor demand the moneys due from Vallejo's proposal. Once again, Vallejo asked to be released from his bond because of "unforeseen embarrassments." He explained in his letter, "My resources and enterprises have been discredited in a great degree from repeated removal of the state archives."

For some time Benicia had been angling for the "capital on wheels." The *Alta California* for December 1852 reported: "A large fine brick edifice has been erected here, intended for a City Hall, but it is

Capitol at Benicia, 1853-1854   *Photo from California Blue Book, 1907*

rumored that strong efforts will be made to induce the Legislature to hold meetings within its walls."

Although other cities made offers, rivalry settled down to San José, Benicia, and Sacramento. San José soon lost ground and sided with Benicia.

Benicia offered "gratuitous use of the City Hall as a State House" plus expenses of moving archives and furniture, just in case the legislature decided on removal.

Sacramento offered the Court House plus expenses of moving both archives and legislators. Sacramento also hired a large steamer, stocked with fancy foods and liquors. At a cost of $13,000, the four days of free food and drink for the lawmakers resulted in a costly disappointment.

The flood of the year before and the disastrous fire that followed made the legislators leery of returning to Sacramento.

Benicia won the battle despite Sacramento's desperate efforts. On February 2nd a bill to provide a permanent location for the seat of government passed the Senate. The bill went to the Assembly the same day together with the opinion of Attorney General

S. C. Hastings: the capital could be removed legally without a two-thirds majority since the original provision related only to San José. On February 4, 1853, the Governor signed the bill making Benicia the "permanent capital" and the legislature ordered adjournment to meet in Benicia on February 11th.

Sacramento took the loss hard, claiming her supposed allies had disobeyed the wishes of their constituents in choosing Benicia.

On the other hand, Benicia's jubilant citizens chartered the steam-tug *Fire-fly* and two scows to move the archives and furniture. Only one slight accident occurred when the safe containing the state's funds slipped from its ropes and crashed to the bottom of the scow. Since there was little gold in the treasury, there was little damage.

Vallejo's settlers followed quickly, leaving only a few stranded inhabitants behind.

Gossip went round that the real reason for the choice of Benicia was the promise to introduce the legislators to twenty or thirty pretty girls of marriageable age. Not so unlikely since in California, at the time, there was one woman to every ten men. A

Benicia Capitol State Historic Park, today.   *Photo from the California Department of Parks and Recreation*

Young Ladies Seminary had opened in 1852 with pupils from the gold mining towns, Hawaii, and even South America. They were instructed in grace and cultural arts. A neat appearance was encouraged, but vanity discouraged with the admonition: "No student is to tarry before a mirror for more than three seconds."

More likely, Benicia's City Hall, above the high water mark, provided the true inducement. The dignified red brick courthouse with its white Doric columns is the only one of California's peripatetic State Houses still extant. Today it is Benicia Capitol State Historic Park.

When the city fathers decided to build, they awarded the job to Reder and Houghton, with a low bid of $24,800. The hurried builders used unburned salmon brick for the exterior walls. They copied from Lefevre's 1833 *Modern Builder's Guide*, choosing the simplest design to create the then fashionable Greek temple effect. Carpenters roofed the classic City Hall with iron plates coated with a composition mixture of lead and tin, called Terne, produced in Wales. Interior wood beams were hand-shaped from masts of aban-

doned sailing vessels. Cornice and moldings were also hand-shaped.

The actual building time, only three months, can be explained by non-existent eight hour days, modern plumbing, heating, lighting, and the red tape of zoning laws. Construction finished right on schedule, January 3, 1853, with keys handed to Mayor Daniel M. Frazer the next day. On February 7th, the Council hurriedly authorized the erection of the almost-overlooked outhouse behind the Capitol building and the flag pole out front.

The Senate settled in the handsome, carpeted Senate Chamber and four large committee rooms on the lower floor. The Assembly occupied the entire 40 by 80 feet second story.

Citizens welcomed the 61 Assemblymen and 39 Senators with a grand complimentary ball, February 9th. A band recruited from Benicia Barracks provided music for dancing in the festively decorated Assembly Hall.

On February 14th, both houses prepared to carry out public business. The *Alta California* (February 5th) expressed sentiments that must have been heartily echoed by everyone: "For the present session...it is to be earnestly hoped that we shall hear no more in the Legislature concerning the removal of the State Capital."

One of the first matters taken up was Vallejo's release from performance of his bond. Vallejo eagerly executed the document releasing himself and the State from damages or any further obligations connected with the seat of government.

On the day after Vallejo signed away the final claim to the capital, William Eames, business representative in Benicia, wrote a letter to Thomas Larkin. It gives insight into the maneuvering that went on and, also, why Vallejo failed:

> I have been very busy since the first of January electioneering for the removal of the seat of Government from Vallejo to Benicia and have at last succeeded it having passed both branches of the Legislature and become a law that Benicia shall be the permanent seat of Government. Acting under the advice of Gen. Estill [also spelled Estell] and others I employed Maj. Graham to remain at Vallejo and "lobby." For this object agreeing to give him $2500 to bring it about. It could not be done without his aid as he had the pledges of a majority of the Senators to go for Vallejo a place he is largely interested. I also agreed to give him (to be deeded to the members they not willing to be known in the transaction) twenty free lots in B_____ but they are mostly of little value. I imagine that Gen. E. gets a large slice of them indirectly....I have paid $1250 to Graham...but lest there might be other influences operating with him between now and the time when the next Legislature meets, I have kept back $1250 until that time, as I have seen enough of late to convince me that trading politicians like him and Gen. E. are not to be trusted.

Estell was one of the men, cooperating with M. G. Vallejo in building the capital city. At the same time he was accepting money for promotion of Benicia. This was not the only instance of his duplicity. Bancroft writes, "Estill [or Estell] was apparently incapable of being honest."

His grand gesture of a glorious capital city brought a hail of criticism to Vallejo. His "scheme" was denounced as donating land "which he did not own and money which he did not have."

Legislative chambers look as they did in 1853-1854

Photo from the California Department of Parks and Recreation

Even those who believed in Vallejo's good intentions classified him as "addicted to idealistic fancies —air castle building or concoction of magnificent schemes and projects difficult of being realized."

The Californios, who had advised Vallejo not to tangle with the shrewd Yankees, felt justified. Vallejo had attained leadership in Mexican California and had fully expected to continue the same role in the new government.

Was there any truth in the criticism hurled at Vallejo? The kernel of truth seems to be that he was no business man and that he put too much trust in others.

Like many Californios, Vallejo suffered financial distress under American administration. When Vallejo returned from imprisonment for two months at Sutter's Fort he wrote Larkin of his losses. He had lost one thousand live horned cattle; six hundred tame horses; his entire wheat crop; estimated at twenty-five thousand bushels, and other valuables. His Indians had disappeared, including faithful Solano. Everything was in shambles. It was the begining of the decline of his fortunes, although he still owned leagues of land, among them the Soscol Grant, site of Vallejo and Benicia.

The Land Commission Act of 1851, sponsored by Senator Gwin, put the burden of proof of land grants on the Californios. Squatters settled on Vallejo's land, defying removal. After three years of litigation both Petaluma and Soscol grants were confirmed.

But squatters, in ascendancy, appealed to the District Court. In 1860, the District Court upheld the action. Again the squatters appealed, this time to the Supreme Court. Finally, came news that the Supreme Court had rejected the Soscol claim on grounds that seem particularly unjust: Governor Micheltorena had the right to give away land but not to sell it.

For years Vallejo had paid expenses for the upkeep of soldiers out of his pocket. Land had been granted him as compensation. In this instance, evidence, in the form of a deed found in the Solano County Court House, shows Micheltorena conveyed the land by deed, not grant, for $5,000. Underhill states, "As far as known this is the only land actually deeded by a governor during either Mexican or Spanish period."

Vallejo had lost several thousand dollars on the shattered dream capital. Greater than the financial loss was the personal defeat, the disappointment in his business partners, and the disillusionment. From then on, Vallejo restricted political office to the local level.

General Vallejo had played a part in the establishment of Benicia, donating the land to Robert Semple, its founder, and Thomas Larkin, its financier. Semple had first glimpsed the beautiful Straits of Carquinez

as a member of the Bear Flag guard escorting Vallejo to imprisonment at Sutter's Fort. The gentle knolls by the bay had immediately impressed him as an ideal site for a city.

Semple, associating with the rough trappers and traders around Sutter's Fort, had picked up their prejudices against the "greasers." On association with Vallejo and other Hispanics, he learned they were cultured gentlemen and quickly changed his opinion.

Vallejo felt much the same way when he first encountered Semple in the Bear Flag Revolt. The Bear Flagger's six-foot six-inch lanky frame was garbed in greasy deerskin trousers, ending at the knee and anchored with loops of string under each foot. The tail of his coonskin cap dangled at the front. As they came to know each other the "Buen Oso" (Good Bear) and General Vallejo became friends.

Vallejo put certain restrictions on the 15 English square miles he donated for Benicia. The city was to be named for his wife. Semple was to establish a ferryboat, proceeds to be retained until the town boasted one hundred families. From then on the income would support public schools.

The survey of Benicia in 1847 covered 2,100 acres. In their plans, the future-minded founders incorporated ideas of modern urban consultants: wide streets, public gardens, four squares for parks and schools—even space for a college. Semple named the city Francisca.

For awhile rivalry between Francisca and Yerba Buena flourished. Alcalde Bartlett felt the name, Yerba Buena, was not sufficiently dignified for a thriving metropolis, and changed the official name to San Francisco.

Luckily, Dona Maria Francisca Felipa Benicia Vallejo had a suffiency of names from which to choose. Semple, to avoid confusion, changed the town's name to Benicia.

Together Semple and Larkin became known as California's first Chamber of Commerce for their successful boosting of Benicia. Larkin's first financial coup involved the Navy. After making soundings of the harbor, Commodore Thomas ap C. Jones purchased twenty-three lots and two business blocks. Next Larkin sold lots to the Army. General Persifer Smith, convinced of Benicia's future, obtained a site for an Army storage depot, bought several lots, and stationed two companies of infantry there. The Pacific Mail Steamship Company established headquarters and berthed its seagoing vessels in Benicia's deepwater harbor.

When the gold rush began, Benicia envisioned unlimited opportunity. At the head of San Francisco Bay, where the Sacramento and San Joaquin Rivers emptied, its site appeared to be a natural trading center. For a time, Semple's erratic, windblown ferry was hard-pressed to keep up with demands for its services. Soon, the rush depleted Benicia, as its inhabitants left for the gold mines and the hordes of miners swept on past.

It was San Francisco where the ships stopped and disgorged their passengers. The bay became a forest of ghostly masts as crews abandoned their ships to join the stampede to the mines. Around the bay grew the saloons, gambling houses, brothels, hotels, and stores.

Semple remained unimpressed by gold. "I'd give more for a good coal mine than all the gold mines in the universe." Obsessed by hopes for Benicia's future, he continued wandering through the streets riding his little white pony, feet dragging the ground.

At the time of its consideration as the capital, the city's population numbered about 1,000. The influx of legislators, state officers, and the inevitable hangers-on brought a bustle of activity and prosperity. Five or six hotels furnished lodgings; grog shops, and other entertainment houses sprung up rapidly. The city fathers made certain a substantial wooden sidewalk extended from the State House to the business district. At last the solons could walk about without muddying their boots.

On February 24th, Mayor David M. Fraser deeded the Benicia City Hall property to the state "for and in consideration of the sum of one dollar, and other good and valuable considerations." Warily, he inserted "for so long as Benicia remained a capital." It was formally accepted by the legislature on May 12th.

On May 18th, the Senate and Assembly passed an act declaring "the city of Benicia situated on the straits of Carquinez shall be and remain the permanent seat of government of California in accordance with the constitution."

The next day the Legislature adjourned. It had considered both continuing and new problems during the fourth session. Governor Bigler had called the attention of the legislature to the need for revision of the act regarding prisons in his annual message. Criminals, attracted to California by gold, made a secure prison a necessity.

M. G. Vallejo and James Estell had been given a contract for guarding, safekeeping, and maintaining state convicts in return for their labor (1851). Requirements called for either the erection of suitable buildings or secure prison ships. Investigation revealed that only one prison brig near Angel Island had been provided. Of sixty prisoners confined, seventeen had escaped, with only a few recaptured.

The controversial policy regarding convicts and the state prison continued throughout Bigler's tenure. A bill for erecting a state prison passed with a limitation of $100,000, but somehow the figure was omitted from the *Journal.* The previous contract was voided and a new bill signed by the Governor, May 11, 1853. Eventually the prison cost the state $153,000.

Another problem that plagued the administration, causing controversy and scandal, was the question of water lots. On Bigler's insistence, the project of extending San Francisco water lots six hundred feet into the bay to raise money for the state treasury was considered. The Governor claimed the state owned title to the lots. San Francisco bitterly opposed the scheme to "cinch" the city and benefit speculators. Those in favor claimed the water-front limits of 1851 were too narrow, the bay too shallow for ocean vessels, and rents too enormous for establishment of new businesses. When the matter came up for final settlement, the vote tied. Lieutenant Governor Purdy cast the deciding vote in favor of postponement, killing the scheme.

Also considered was a plan requiring miners to secure fee simple titles to their claims as a means of taxing the gold fields. It was decided to continue as before with the customs and regulations made by the miners themselves in force and mines open to all enterprising individuals.

A precedent-setting case came up in the Senate on the petition of James Burdue, convicted for crimes for which he was innocent. He claimed $4,000 in reimbursement for expenses. The judiciary committee differed, stating, "He should rejoice that the laws have afforded protection to him when wrongfully accused, rather than seek renumeration for his expenses from the government whose justice has protected him from ignominious death." James Stuart, who actually committed the crimes, had been executed by the Vigilance Committee. To reimburse persons prosecuted and acquitted for crime would have strained the state's treasury.

Another matter that came up before the Senate was the division of the state into two or more parts. Southern landowners complained about the inequalities of taxation. There was also talk of a convention, one purpose being revision of the tax laws. After much discussion the resolution was tabled.

Many of the emigrants to California heartily agreed with the legislature's request that Governor Bigler confer the honorary rank of Major General of the California Militia on John Sutter—recognition of his generosity to American pioneers. Strategically located on the Sacramento River, Sutter's Fort was the objective of wagon parties traveling overland or coming from Oregon. Here the weary, often half-starved emigrants found succor, solace, and employment.

Sutter had wrested an empire from the wilderness. Genial, hospitable, filled with expansive ambitions,

Sutter's enterprises multiplied but never quite caught up with his debts. Ironically, gold discovery brought disaster. He was unable to cope with the onslaught of squatters who invaded his vast acreage; unable to grasp the new opportunities.

The legislature commissioned William S. Jewett to paint Sutter's portrait for $5,000 and displayed it prominently at the Capitol. At the time, Sutter was 50-years old, already a "living artifact" of an era that ended with the gold rush.

Citizens took an avid interest in the act authorizing the capture of outlaws that had robbed, killed, and terrorized the entire Mother Lode. On May 17, 1853, the legislature asked bounty hunter, Captain Harry Love, to form a band of 20 State Rangers to kill or capture any of five bandits—all named Joaquin—within three months. To the Ranger's generous pay of $150 a month, Governor Bigler added a $1,000 reward.

Time was running out when the tough California Rangers rode into the bandit camp headed by notorious Joaquin Murieta. The posse subdued the desperados after a short skirmish. Love ordered Joaquin's head chopped off, along with the hand of his accomplice, vicious Three-fingered Jack, and pickled the evidence in a keg of whisky.

The grisly trophies were exhibited statewide. A grateful legislature awarded an additional $5,000 to Captain Love in 1854, although Captain Byrnes was in command at the time of capture.

Was it Joaquin Murieta's head? Opinions differed. The poster accompanying the exhibit stated: "It was recognized by hundreds of people." A lady, supposedly Joaquin's sister, said, "I don't know who it is; but it isn't Joaquin."

The *Alta California* in its story on August 23, 1853, declared the whole affair a "humbug." The head recently exhibited in Stockton bears no resemblance to that individual, and this is positively asserted by those who have seen the real Murieta and his spurious head!"

Whatever the truth, legend has transformed Murieta into a Robin Hood-type folk-hero who stole from the rich "gringos" to give to the poor Mexicans.

Speaker of the Assembly Isaac B. Wall startled the legislature in his farewell address. He castigated the "scheming for private gain" endemic in the legislature. He described Democracy as something that is honorable, noble, elevated—" something that demanded personal sacrifices...a something which could not live without patriotism, or exist without love for one's fellow-man."

The Democratic Party, influenced by Broderick, nominated Bigler for Governor again in 1853.

The platform consisted of nothing more than "glit-

Sutter dressed in elaborate army uniform for his portrait as honorary Major General of the California Militia.
Photo from the California State Library

tering generalities." A group of Democratic seceders, calling themselves a reform party, canvassed the state in an impassioned campaign against Bigler. William Waldo, a Whig known for his integrity, ran as his opponent and was said to be favored.

No one could beat the Broderick-Bigler combination. Bigler won a second term with a majority of 1,503 votes. To win Broderick used foul as well as fair means. The Governor won by five votes in San Francisco where he met strong opposition because of his advocacy of the Water Lot Bill. According to Bancroft, "$1,500,000 in money and water lots" were used to tip the vote in Bigler's favor. Additionally, steamer tickets bribed several hundred miners returning to the states to vote the right way.

The mechanics of party politics made chicanery easy. Parties printed and distributed their own distinctively colored ballots and provided their own poll watchers. Since there was no Great Register of Voters in the counties until 1866 or secret ballot until 1891, parties voted their members "early and often...as well as voting the passenger lists from passing steamboats and stagecoaches." Names from tombstone lists also came in handy.

In Los Angeles, men stuffed the ballot box by going through several times in different disguises. Broderick, always open in discussing his devious methods, defended his use of hooligans, "You respectable people I can't depend on. You won't go down and face the revolvers of those fellows; and I have to take such material as I can get hold of. They stuff ballot boxes, and steal tally lists; and I have to keep these fellows to aid me."

David C. Broderick's single goal in life was to become a United States Senator. Reelection of Bigler as Governor removed him as candidate for Senator. The race for United States Senator also became intertwined with removal of the capital to Sacramento in 1854.

CHAPTER IX

Sacramento:
The Permanent Seat of Government
Fifth Session: 1854

When the legislature met January 2, 1854, the movement for removal had been gathering momentum for three months. Sacramento determined to wrest the capital from Benicia with whatever steps were necessary. In one sly, well-thought-out action, two to three hundred young Sacramento men appropriated hotel and boarding house rooms before the lawmakers arrived.

Once again the waspish legislators aired familiar complaints about scarcity of accommodations, exorbitant prices, and lack of improvements during the year.

This time agitation for removal started with Governor Bigler's annual message. The Governor began on an encouraging note: "All the sources of wealth have been greatly augmented by the enterprise and well directed efforts of our people." He lapsed immediately into a doleful analysis of state debt, three million in arrears with an expected expenditure of another million. Projected revenues amounted to only eight hundred thousand.

Again, although fully aware of San Francisco's opposition, Bigler strongly advocated the extension and sale of water lots as the foolproof solution to wiping out all debt and acquiring a surplus. For the most part, the Governor restated old views. He termed the squatters "that enterprising and useful portion of our people." In cases where settlers made honest mistakes in preemption of claims, he recommended compensation for their improvements. He believed the federal government should remove Indians from the state and was against the sale or lease of mineral land.

The Governor lost no time in introducing the question of removal: "I feel it incumbent upon me to direct your attention to the insecure position of the public archives. The entire public records as well as the State Library, now about four thousand volumes, are kept in fragile frame buildings without fireproof vaults." He suggested measures be taken for their security immediately.

Two days later, Bigler (a Sacramentan) followed through with a special message transmitting a communication from the Mayor and Common Council of Sacramento offering:

> to grant to the State government the free use of the court-house and other suitable rooms, for the accommodation of the State officers, together with fire-proof vaults for the security of the public moneys and records; to remove the members of the Legislature and State officers and the government furniture and archives, free of charge, from Benicia; and to grant to the State, for a building lot for the capitol, the public square between I and J and Ninth and Tenth streets.

Benicia fought back with a counter offer of free use of buildings occupied by the state as long as they were needed. They also offered to donate additional lots for public buildings.

For the moment, attention turned to the ceremonies attendant on the Governor's inaugural. On January 7th Bigler arrived at Benicia's harbor on the

Senator accompanied by a crowd of admirers and the San Francisco Blues, a crack military organization. A procession escorted the Governor to the State House. When His Excellency walked down the passageway lined with Blues and was announced by the sergeant-at-arms, the entire Senate and Assembly rose to their feet. After the oath of office for the second term was administered, the Governor made his inaugural address.

As always at the beginning of each session, the attention of the lawmakers revolved around the capital. According to the usual procedure, the Committee on Public Buildings and Grounds in each house did the committee work before discussion. This time after accepting the Governor's message, a select committee was appointed for study of the problem.

On January 13th the House committee announced inability to make an unanimous report. Chairman S. A. Ballou (El Dorado) reported for the majority, favoring removal to Sacramento. He praised Sacramento for its rapid rebuilding after the flood and disastrous fire of 1852.

Sacramento deserved praise. On the night of November 4th, fire broke out in a millinery shop. The gale-whipped blaze raced through the city, engulfing the frail wooden homes and businesses. By morning two-thirds of the city was a black desolate wasteland, with damages an estimated six million, its 12,000 population virtually homeless.

Two years later, as the legislature convened, the city boasted several hundred brick buildings. There were new levees, and raised streets covered with wooden planks. Stage lines offered transport to the interior and magnificent steamboats plied between San Francisco and the northern cities on the Sacramento River.

Ballou pointed out, "Benicia had neither the necessary printing press or law library. Besides removal at the cost of $15,000 would be considerably cheaper than staying in Benicia."

In conclusion, he stated, "In the location of the State Capitol your committee is of the opinion that public convenience and public economy should be the controlling considerations, in fact they are indispensable to a final and permanent settlement of the question..."

The minority, represented by Henry Kellog (Yuba) and Bernard Whitman (Solano) refuted the arguments. They maintained Benicia had four thousand books in the library, a brick building in process of construction that could easily be made fire-proof, and the cost of removal would top $15,000.

They offered statistics as to removal costs:

Release of present State House	$27,000.00
Per diem of legislature—	
7 days of adjournment	14,000.00
Extra mileage	4,472.00
Damage to furniture by moving	1,000.00
	$46,472.00

The committee quoted the report of the Comptroller, who had been directed to submit the cost of past removals:

From Monterey to San Jose	$ 1,100.00
From San Jose to Vallejo	57,419.04
From Vallejo to San Jose	348.00 [archives]
From San Jose to Vallejo	8,064.00
From Vallejo to Sacramento	13,159.50
From Sacramento to Vallejo	1,100.00
From Vallejo to Benicia	12,000.00
	$93,190.54

Early in the session, resolutions offered on the floor failed; for a while it looked as if Benicia would triumph. On February 3rd, Assemblyman Springer again introduced the bill for removal—the resolution carried, only to be defeated in the Senate. James Coffroth argued fervently that constant moving damaged California's reputation and made her a figure of ridicule in addition to being expensive.

As the balloting went on a flurry of offers besieged the legislature from Stockton, Nevada City, Mokelumne Hill, and others.

Columbia would have been included in the list but for a bizarre, half-legendary incident. Richard Dillon recounts the episode in *Great Expectations*, the story of Benicia. Supposedly, 10,000 Columbians signed the petition to transfer the capital to the "Gem of the Southern Mines." For utmost security, the document was locked in a bank vault.

Meanwhile, Peter Nicholas and John Parrott became embroiled in a violent argument, resulting in the knifing and death of Parrott. A mob of miners, intent on hanging him, strung Nicholas to the nearest tree, but the branch broke. The sheriff rescued Nicholas, choking but alive—in the nick of time—and threw him in jail.

Nicholas was tried and sentenced to death legally. However, he possessed steadfast, powerful, and intrepid friends, among them his attorney, Horace Bull, and Senator Coffroth. One of them slipped into the vault, stole the petition, and changed it into a pardon plea for the convicted man.

When Governor Bigler received the petition, he cancelled the death sentence immediately and without question. A man who had 10,000 friends controlled as many votes.

A slightly different version reports the document was steamer bound for Benicia from Stockton. Friends of Nicholas aboard mourned his projected death in a drinking bout, when hit with an inspired

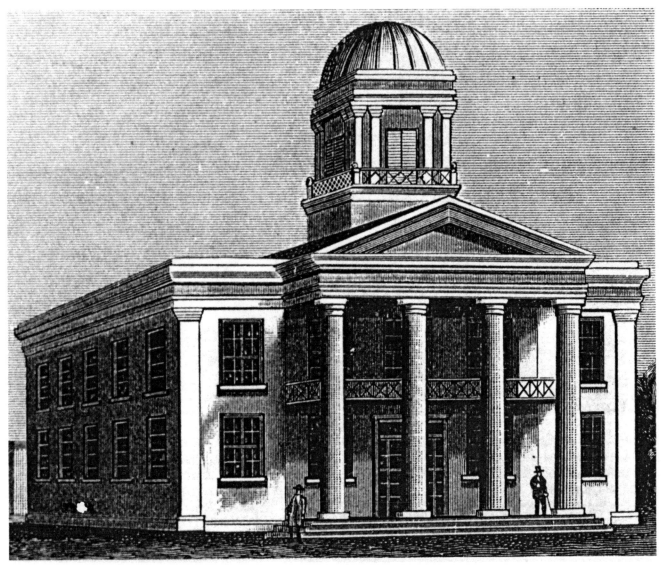

The original state Capitol at Sacramento, 1854.   *Photo from California Blue Book, 1907*

way of saving his life. The altered document served its purpose; Nicholas served four years for manslaughter. Columbia lost all chance for the capital.

An unprecedented tug-of-war developed between the forces favoring the Sacramento capital and the foes. The removal of the capital had become embroiled in the political ambitions of State Senator David C. Broderick.

Schooled in politics in New York's Tammany Hall, Broderick came to California fired with one purpose. Reportedly, he once told a friend, "to sit in the Senate of the United States as a Senator for one day, I would consent to be roasted in a slow fire on the plaza."

Young Broderick, only twenty-nine years old, arrived in San Francisco ill and penniless. He swiftly built a fortune from investment, on borrowed money, in a private mint in partnership with Fredrick D. Kohler, a political associate from New York. The

coins sold for $5 and $10, although actual value in gold dust was $4 to $8. The immense profits, invested in San Francisco water lots spiraled into a fortune. Broderick used the money to further his political ends.

A paradox of a man—austere, dignified, temperate, in private life, Broderick used his leisure to study history and politics. In politics, he had few compunctions in reaching his objectives.

Broderick never lost sight of his ambitions, channeling all his energies and manipulative talents toward his single-minded goal of becoming Senator. A candidate for the Senate in 1852, he lost to John Weller. Broderick then made up his mind to take William Gwin's place. Gwin's term was to expire March 3, 1855.

Broderick schemed to have the election take place a year earlier in 1854 by a legislature which had no right to elect. There was no law against the practice and

Sacramento in 1850. (From the original lithograph.)   Courtesy of the Sacramento Museum and History Department

Broderick forces contended there could be a deadlock in 1855. Sides were drawn up for and against the unorthodox election. Conflicts intensified; instances of bribery multiplied.

Every vote for Broderick's scheme counted. It mattered not a whit to Broderick whether Sacramento was the capital or not. To a number of his supporters, Sacramento's destiny as a capital was of vital importance. It became understood that the price of a vote for the capital was a vote for Broderick's project.

As the election contest went on, a new bill to locate the capital at Sacramento was introduced into the Senate. It passed and was rushed into the Assembly, friendly to Broderick, on February 24, 1854. The next day, Governor Bigler signed the bill into law. The same day, both houses adopted a concurrent resolution to adjourn and meet at Sacramento, March 1, 1854.

On the 28th of February, the *Wilson G. Hunt*, with Governor Bigler, the State officers, legislators, and a committee of Sacramento citizens aboard steamed into the Embarcadero. On the levee, several thousand citizens cheered a welcome. Sutter's Rifles escorted the Governor and party to the Orleans Hotel. Oratory flowed in addresses of welcome answered by the Governor and other state officials.

On March 6, 1854, Broderick's battle for the election change continued on a higher level of desperation. The Assembly passed the bill in the morning, 41-38.

In the afternoon, suspense charged the Senate chambers. A crowd of spectators as well as the entire Assembly watched. Broderick stood, with clenched fists, his face inscrutable. The Senators answered to the roll call, each voting as expected, except for Jacob Grewell, a Santa Clara clergyman. He voted for the election bill, tying the vote, 17-17. Lieutenant Governor Samuel Purdy cast the deciding vote for the election. Broderick's followers gathered around, congratulating him on his triumph in a tumult of cheering, shouting and exultation.

The triumph was reversed the next day. Grewell lacked the integrity to stay bought. Opposition forces persuaded him to move for reconsideration, which was carried out in the Assembly and rejected in the Senate. The second day the entire subject was postponed indefinitely as was the move to reconsider. Broderick's chances for election were postponed also. His defeat fueled his unswerving ambition and he was finally elected Unites States Senator in 1857.

Sacramento had won the hard fought battle for the capital. Bancroft quotes the *San Francisco Post*, April 14, 1877:

> A writer says that he was told by a shrewd and wily politician that to secure the passage of the bill removing the capital to Sac.[ramento], he paid $10,000 in gold to the reigning king of the lobby, with which to purchase the votes of ten senators, and that the money was paid over for that purpose, and secured the measure. Though many of our patriots who go to Sacra-

mento to make laws can be bought for $200 to $300, as high as $50,000 has been paid for a single vote.

No longer would the capital be hawked about for sale to the highest bidder.

Yet, that same year Sacramento came close to losing the capital. On March 24, 1854, an act ordered the Supreme Court to hold its sessions in the legal seat of government.

The Supreme Court, bewildered by frequent juggling of the legal seat, refused to obey the law and remained in San Francisco. The majority, Justices Heydenfelt and Wells, declared San José the legal capital, Justice Murray dissenting.

The majority argued that the Constitution of 1849 providing for the removal of the seat of government by two-thirds of both houses of the legislature applied to all removals. In the dissenting opinion, Chief Justice Hugh C. Murray contended removal power belonged solely to the legislature. It could not be taken over by a judicial power—even to determine legality.

San Joseans maintained that when Vallejo failed to fulfill his promises, the capital should have reverted to San José automatically, Citizens expressed delight in recapturing the capital.

Alta California (March 29, 1854) declared that if the legislature must sit at San José, the legal seat of government, then all subsequent legislation was void and this would lead to litigation. The editor suggested an easy solution: The present legislature should declare Sacramento the seat of government by a two-thirds majority.

The Supreme Court directed the sheriff of Santa Clara County to procure and furnish a court house and clerks' office. The judicial archives were moved on the 30th.

On July 13th an event occurred which increased San José's confidence. A great fire swept through Sacramento destroying much of the business district and the Court House. The next day the *Democratic State Journal* reported on Governor Bigler's participation in saving the furniture.

When the fire threatened the courthouse with destruction, the Governor (Bigler), who was present and who had been working from the commencement of the fire wherever Sacramento most needed a soldier, asked those present to assist him in saving the furniture. To this many objected, on the ground that private parties, who could not suffer the loss as well as the county, needed their services. A full-length portrait of Washington was standing against the southern wall, and pointing to it, the Governor said, 'See, there is the portrait of the father of your country; will you permit it to be destroyed?' when a general rush was made for the portrait, and it was saved.

Immediately, while blackened timbers still smoked,

the county contracted for a larger and more impressive courthouse on the same site. The ground floor housed the county prison. The same floor contained offices for the State Controller and State Treasurer and the all-important fireproof vaults. The second floor provided chambers for the Senate and Assembly and nine rooms for clerks and committees. Originally, the county planned to spend $100,600, but the total cost escalated to $240,000.

Since the Supreme Court had declared San José the legal seat of government, Thomas Vermeule and other San Joseans filed a test suit to determine judicially the location of the capital.

Judge Craven Hester, of the third judicial district, upheld the Supreme Court decision and issued a mandate "directing State officers to show cause why they should not forthwith remove their officers and papers to San José."

The opening of the next legislature was only a month away. No one knew for certain where it would meet. It was anticipated that state officers would appeal Judge Hester's decision to the Supreme court.

In the meantime, work continued on the prospective capitols in Sacramento and San Jose. Newspaper accounts explained the peculiar situation.

In Sacramento, the *Daily Union*, December 17, 1854 reported:

The work on the Capitol continues with unremitted vigor. In the Assembly Chamber the plastering is completed, the floors laid, and the remainder of the woodwork completed. The plastering of the Senate Chamber was finished yesterday, and the scaffolding removed preparatory to laying floors today.

On the same day the *San José Tribune* described San José's projected capitol:

The new City Hall progressing rapidly, and will be completed by Christmas. We will know sometime next week, whether it will be required by the Legislature, or whether we will be chiseled out of our rights by the unscrupulous and ambitious neighbor, as it is generally understood that the Supreme Court will hold an extra session to determine the mandamus.

And again on December 25th, the *San José Telegraph* wrote:

In view on the roof of the Capitol, we counted twenty-one men at work—how many more there were out of sight, engaged in work upon it, we cannot say. The front of the Capitol, as we said, is very beautiful and imposing. It looks quite as well from the street as the bogus one at Sacramento does in the picture.

Both edifices were constructed for other uses as a precaution: The one in Sacramento for a Court House; San José's intended Capitol on Market Street as a City Hall.

State officers appealed Judge Hester's decision to the Supreme Court, December 28, 1854. For Sacramento's purposes the timely death of Supreme Court Justice Alexander Wells was a factor in settling the matter. Bigler appointed Charles H. Bryan to replace Wells. Bryan joined with Justice Murray to reverse the decision. Sacramento—not San José—was the legal seat of government. Disgruntled, San Joseans felt Bigler had chosen Justice Bryan (Yuba) deliberately for his sympathy with Sacramento.

Repeated calamities of flood and fire failed to intimidate Sacramento's dauntless citizens. After each catastrophe the city came back stronger.

Three months after laying the cornerstone with Masonic honors, the Court House was completed. The building became the State House when the legislature convened in January 1855. The state rented the building for $12,000 annually, later decreased to $8,000, until moving to the new Capitol in 1869.

Sacramento, the "Gateway to the Gold Fields," was a thriving commercial city of some 13,000 people. The Sierra diggings still yielded treasure of $3,000,000 in gold yearly.

The city had sprung up around Sutter's Embarcadero, when the rush of gold seekers stimulated a flourishing trade. Captain John Sutter, as a ploy against pressing creditors, had deeded power-of-attorney to his son, John Augustus Sutter, Jr. Sensing opportunity, young Sutter had a city laid out and engaged Peter Burnett, later governor, as agent for sale of his lots.

Sacramento grew with a virility that tests belief. In August 1849, William L. Schooning wrote:

> The place is eight weeks old and now has upwards of 1,000 houses, wholesale and retail stores, daily auction houses; in fact it has every appearance of a flourishing city. Houses are principally made of canvas cloth, though there are going up a great many fine frame buildings. The sound of the hammer and saw is heard in every direction. You can form no correct idea how things appear, indeed its more like a romance or dream than Reality.

Despite its propensity for moving, the "floating" capital remained in Sacramento, except for a few months in 1862 when a flood drove the legislature to San Francisco. The handsome Court House/State House with its portico supported by ten massive Ionic pillars served the legislature for fifteen years.

Capitol at Sacramento during the inauguration of Governor John B. Weller, January 8, 1858. (From a photograph by W. Dickman, Sacramento.)

Courtesy of Sacramento Museum and History Department

CHAPTER X
A Capitol of Its Own: The Beginnings
Reuben Clark's Contribution

The Court House was never intended to be a permanent Capitol. State offices were inconvenienced by the need to find accommodations in the business district. By 1856, general opinion conceded; "the courthouse building was too small." Besides, dignity and economy demanded that a great state own its Capitol outright rather than paying $12,000 annual rental.

The legislature passed a bill (April 18, 1856), providing for a Capitol to rise in a public square between I and J and Ninth and Tenth that had been deeded to Sacramento by John Sutter, Jr. A Board of Capitol Commissioners was to make contracts and supervise building. The cost, limited to $300,000, was to be paid for by thirty-year bonds.

The Board chose plans submitted by Reuben Clark. The edifice, Corinthian in style, formed a Greek cross. The building was to be 312 feet long and 145 feet wide, some four times larger than the Court House. The rooms were commodious with a second story circular Senate chamber rising 36 feet. The large Assembly hall was 84 by 52 1/2 feet. The library location on the second floor made research convenient. Committee rooms occupied the third floor. A stately dome 132 feet from the ground and a rotunda 40 feet in diameter and 118 feet in height were part of the design.

The contract was let to Joseph Nougues, builder of the 1855 courthouse, for $200,000. Nougues staked off the ground and started building the foundation on December 2, 1856. He was to be paid in bonds as work progressed. However, state officers refused to issue

the money on the grounds that the bonds were in excess of the amount permitted by the Constitution.

Nougues took the matter to the Supreme Court, but the case was decided against him. The legislature finally paid the Nougues claim for $5,388.05 in labor and materials in 1859. Work stopped and never resumed. The square turned back into a public park, now Plaza Park.

As state business increased, the need for a new Capitol became even more apparent. Governor Neely Johnson in his annual message (1858) called attention to the fact that "after frequent changes" the government had at last attained "a degree of permanency." A Capitol for California made good financial sense as well as being a matter of pride. Rent paid over the years equalled the cost of a suitable building. He recommended an appropriation of $100,000 a year for three years to finance a first class Capitol.

In February 1858, a joint committee investigated purchase of the courthouse Capitol. Senator William Ferguson introduced the bill to purchase the building for the amount agreed to by Sacramento's supervisors, $125,000, which was referred to the Committee on Public Buildings.

The majority report favored the bill. The dissenting minority pointed out disadvantages and alternate plans: (1) The state-owned square of land, valued at $40,000, would revert to the city unless used, (2) The state already owned plans for a Capitol, (3) Prison labor could quarry and prepare granite and also

Reuben Clark's conception of the Capitol. From Clark's watercolor.   Photo from the California Department of Parks and Recreation

manufacture brick, holding costs for the capitol to $200,000, (4) The present Capitol had been erected hastily as a courthouse and was dilapidated and disintegrating. To remodel it would be more expensive than erecting a new building.

The Senate considered the matter until the end of the session, when it was tabled.

The old image of a roving capital had not been erased. A movement to remove the capital to Oakland burgeoned in 1858. A memorial from the Mayor, Council, and citizens of Oakland was presented in the Senate and Assembly. A joint investigation committee reported back that Oakland citizens offered to furnish suitable buildings at a nominal rental until erection of a Capitol, and to donate a 20-acre site for public buildings.

In the Assembly's opinion, the Oakland site was superior to that of Sacramento: they recommended removal. The Senate concurred, but made no recommendation. The bill met with defeat.

A substitute bill authorized a fund to build a Capitol at Oakland: funds to be raised by $10 on each $100 of Oakland city real estate and 50 cents on every

$100 of Alameda County real estate. Also a donation of 10 acres of land would be used for the site. A bill was introduced to appropriate $200,000 for erection of a Capitol at Oakland. Both bills were defeated.

Governor Weller in his annual message in 1860 recommended the state appropriate $100,000 for a new Capitol as an economy move to avoid rental. It seemed like old times with Oakland, San Francisco, San José, and Sacramento anxious to be considered for the Capitol.

An act to remove the Capital to Oakland, if the city donated a quantity of land was referred to a select committee. San Francisco offered any public square (except Portsmouth) and city bonds to $150,000 as long as the capital stayed in the city. Citizens of San José, once again, renewed their claim that removal from the city was unconstitutional. Sacramento offered free use of the Court House to the legislators.

The committee visited the cities and made a lengthy report. Three members recommended removal to San Francisco. Four recommended immediate construction of a Capitol in Sacramento.

Discussion occupied days before approval of the

Mixing cement by horsepower.   *Photo from the California State Library, circa 1870*

final bill for construction of the Capitol. Governor Downey signed on March 29, 1860. The law provided for a commission to superintend and contract for the construction of the building, limited to $500,000. The city of Sacramento deeded the major portion of four large blocks, L to N and Tenth to Twelfth. The state condemned the remainder for $65,517.

The land was appraised by the special commission. People had to be moved. Houses, fruit trees, outbuildings and fences were sold at auction September 1, 1860. Money collected was credited toward the State Capitol.

The auction had its heartrending moments. When auctioneer, C. H. Grimm, offered Mrs. Hanks' house for sale, she appeared on the steps. Between copious tears and sad wails, she declared, "My home is being sold without my consent." Spectators were sympathetic. The house was sold back to the tearful lady for $117 without contest; it had been assessed at $800.

Even after several more auctions, money to pay the property owners was short. Merchants, particularly D. O. Mills, made up the difference.

The state had problems with owners who ignored

eviction notices. Three years later, the Sacramento County Hospital was still there. The Commissioners began ejection action against the County of Sacramento.

Seven architects competed for the $1,500 prize for the best design. Miner F. Butler's plan won on the fifth ballot, receiving the award. Butler's plan, by happenstance or design, closely followed the one submitted by Clark in 1856. Some historians believe Clark made the major contribution and should have received the prize.

Reuben Clark, employed by Butler, became Superintending Architect. From Maine, Clark had experience on the commission for the Mississippi State Capitol.

Work commenced on the new Capitol quickly. The city council closed streets and alleys.

The immense weight of the building required monolithic foundations. Laborers dug trenches and filled them with a layer of rock. The concrete mix consisted of cement together with broken rock and gravel "varying from the size of a pigeon's egg to that of a hen's egg." This was poured over the rock bed in one foot layers, to a depth of three feet. By May, nearly one half of the foundation, some 1,800 yards, was completed.

A 42 foot square shed housed the mixing of the mortar for construction of the basement walls. Lime, sand, and water were placed in a circular pit and mixed by means of a wooden wheel turned by horses walking the circle.

The cornerstone was laid with proper Masonic ceremonies on May 15, 1861 before a crowd of prominent people. Ten workmen had spent five days preparing for the occasion, leveling the ground and building platforms covered with awnings for seating—one for the officials, legislators, and state officers; another for the ladies. Three thousand spectators came by foot, horseback, and carriage. San Francisco Masons came on the river steamer "Antelope."

The procession to the Capitol from the Masonic Hall on J Street started an hour and a half late, delaying the ceremonies. The Union Guard gave the salute in honor of the day by "explosions from well-rammed cartridges" of muzzle-loaded rifles. Banners and flags, in festive profusion, bedecked platforms, unfurled from flagpoles, appeared even in the aprons worn by pert young ladies.

S. M. Wilson, an attorney from San Francisco, gave the oration address. The long list of objects, stuffed into the copper basket for the benefit of future generations, was read. Among the documents and artifacts deemed worthy of inclusion: The Constitution of the United States, Seal of California, bylaws of several Masonic Lodges, City Directory of Sacramento for 1861, daily newspapers, Holy Bible, $3 issued by the Continental Congress at Philadelphia, lithographs of the proposed Capitol, various coins and stamps, a

silver plate with the words, "This cornerstone laid by the Most Worshipful N. Greene Curtis, Grand Master of the Masons, May 15, A. L. 1861."

The Grand Master expressed his hopes: "May this building be speedily completed; may symmetry and order rest upon each line and curve; may strength and beauty characterize each arch and pillar."

Officials lowered the casket into the prepared cavity at the northeast corner. Pouring the ceremonial corn, wine, and oil on top, Curtis intoned, "May all-wise, bountiful Providence grant to the people of this commonwealth an abundance of the corn of nourishment, the wine of refreshment, and the oil of Joy."

According to the *Sacramento Union* account, the celebration ended with a banquet that lasted until 1 a.m.

Work went on in fits and starts as one contractor quit and another contract was let. New contractors faced cement shortages on the local market. Sacramento Valley Railroad refused to deliver granite from Folsom unless the freight bill was paid on the spot. The capitol contractor was charged $3.00 per ton. Rates to San Francisco were only $1.50. The reason given by the railroad: "In San Francisco they had to compete with vessels arriving from China. There was no incentive to give favors in Sacramento." They added, "They had a legal right to charge double rates."

On December 9, 1861, a flood inundated the city leaving capitol foundations weakened.

The thirteenth session of the legislature met in Sacramento, January 6, 1862. On the day of Governor-Elect Leland Stanford's inaugural,

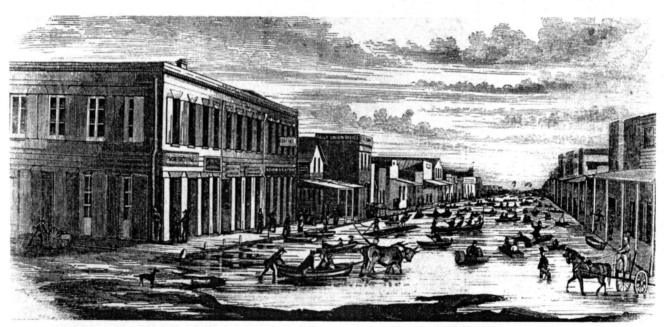

The flood at Sacramento City, California—view on J Street.   Courtesy of the Sacramento Museum and History Department

January 10th, the city was visited with the worst flood in its flood-prone history.

Water, yellowed by mining debris, swirled around the Stanford mansion. Stanford and his party had to be rowed to the Capitol in boats. On his return, the Governor found the first floor submerged, the piano floating about the reception room. He climbed into the house through a second-story window.

The legislature arranged for hard-to-get rowboats to transport their members to and from the Capitol. One Senator declared, "I think I'm doing my whole duty when I eat one meal a day—cold at that—in a garret and shin down an awning to get into a boat." Hotel dining rooms had closed. Many subsisted on cheese and crackers.

The *Sacramento Union* wailed about another inconvenience: "The little buildings in the backyards are overwhelmed with mud."

One politician worried about the legislature's image "as the changing mudscow, steamboat moving, forever uncertain legislature of California."

Steamers from San Francisco brought emergency supplies of hot food, dry clothing, and rowboats along with crews. They chugged across the 60-mile Sacramento Valley, now a lake, avoiding floating fragments of houses, trees, and furniture.

Rainfall in the winter of 1861-62 measured 27 inches above normal—24.36 inches fell in January alone.

Newspapers statewide predicted Sacramento's demise. The *San Francisco Call* opined: "It is simply an act of folly for the people of the town of Sacramento to endeavor to maintain their city on its present location." The *Nevada Transcript* was blunt: "Sacramento is a doomed city."

With the Capitol afloat, the Senate adopted a concurrent resolution to meet in San Francisco for the remainder of the session. The Assembly refused to concur by a narrow margin. Arguments of legality raged. Continued uncomfortable conditions, the aftermath of sludgy floodwaters, and the Attorney General's opinion that a move for one session would not violate the Constitution overcame the Assembly's reluctance.

Sacramentans, fearful that the move to San Francisco might be permanent, felt threatened. The *Sacramento Union* chastized the Governor in print for not exerting sufficient pressure to keep the legislature in their city. Others came to his defense with the reminder that "the Governor's home, business interests, and loyalties centered in Sacramento."

As rumors circulated that the flood had undermined the Capitol foundations, offers inundated the legislature. Acts to relocate the capital were introduced. Once again San José offered the use of its City Hall. Efforts to keep the legislature in San Francisco failed.

By March, Sacramento began the slow process of drying out. Judge Fields scraped two feet of mud out of the parlor of his house situated on high ground. Most of the streets became passable. But the Capitol and the Governor's mansion still stood in a lake.

The flood set back capitol construction. Clark reported work must be resumed at once. Laborers should be hired to open drains, clear standing water, and mix mortar. The 1,100 barrels of lime could be salvaged if immediately mixed with sand and made into mortar. Clark said, "The foundations are secure and have not been damaged by flood."

Contractors quit, complaining of financial loss. One foot of water and mud surrounded foundations. The flood had swept away 1000 barrels of lime, 200 barrels of cement and a large quantity of lumber. Granite could not be transported, since the Sacramento Valley Railroad was inoperable. In April, the Commission cancelled the contract after awarding builders $55,570.26 to pay for labor, materials and flood damage.

Work continued sporadically on a day labor basis. The Commissioners modified plans so that costs would not exceed $500,000. No general contractors were used on the remainder of the building.

Yet, optimism swelled with the shrinking waters. The *Union* referred to Sacramento's miraculous resurgence from the ashes after disastrous fires. Then predicted, "beautiful as Venus she will now rise from the waves."

Sacramento had long known levee improvements and filling the streets to higher grade were overdue. The flood of 1861-62 gave impetus to the task. Sacramento literally lifted itself by its bootstraps, high grading the streets by twelve feet. Buildings either had to be raised by dozens of jack screws or buried so first floors became basements. It took tons and tons of filler, $200,000, and Herculean effort. An incredible achievement!

The Capitol under construction was raised thirteen feet in two wide terraces, burying the cornerstone underground. Also, flood stains had marred the granite walls. Workers went about redressing them resignedly.

Governor Stanford in his annual message, December 1863, reported work on the Capitol had resumed within the limits of state appropriations. He recommended issuance of bonds to hasten construction. He stated, "In a young state like our own, poor in comparison with what its future promises, future generations should share with the present in the erection of any great and permanent building. The State capitol of California, that is to endure for generations, should be a structure that the future will be proud of, and surrounded by grounds that should extend into the dimensions of an ample park."

Although a number of bills for funds were introduced in 1863, none received approval. Still work went forward slowly with a special Capitol Fund of 5 cents on every $100 of property, later increased to 10 cents.

Frederick Lux made an effort to solve funding problems January 5, 1864. His Assembly bill requested the State to issue bonds for $1,000,000, proceeds to be used for immediate completion of the Capitol. The lengthy debate ended March 16th, when the bill was postponed indefinitely.

Original specifications had called for granite for its sturdiness and inherent beauty. Quarried near Folsom it was delivered by barge down the American and Sacramento Rivers or by the Sacramento Valley Railroad. Even before completion of the first floor, it was decided to use hard-burned brick covered with mastic (plaster), in place of hard-to-transport granite.

Brief strikes interrupted work. If workmen had received wages in gold, they would have had no quarrel with the rate of pay: $3 for unskilled laborers; $4.50-$5.50 for carpenters, brickmasons, and teamsters. Instead they were paid in state scrip of fluctuating value.

Weather also caused a problem. Work stopped in the wettest months. Shade for the 35 stonecutters and plentiful ice were necessities in scorching summers. A bill records payment for 9,243 pounds of ice one August.

The Civil War contributed to shortage of materials and complicated delivery. Many items had to be made in San Francisco where facilities and materials were limited. The massive wrought iron beams had to be shipped around the Horn. Without supporting beams, there could be no floors. In 1865 Clark still waited.

The principal reason for lack of progress was simply inadequate funding. The fact that the legislature met for two months only every other year contributed to uncertain appropriations.

Clark had 54 men in his employ. He needed four or five times that many workers to speed up building. By 1865, walls had risen to twelve feet, giving at least the look of progress. An intrepid lady, who believed the flag should be flying over the unfinished building, took action. She confiscated two of the workmen's ladders and placed the flag atop the walls. She left a note signed, "A poor but patriotic woman." The workmen quickly constructed a 75 foot flag pole. From that day on the Stars and Stripes flew over the Capitol.

Architect Clark had served efficiently and conscientiously in spite of continuous frustrations. Exhausted physically and mentally, he was given a leave of absence in September 1865. He was admitted to Stockton State Hospital in February 1866 and died there in July of that year.

Hospital records give the cause of Clark's mental illness as "continued and close attention to the building of the State Capitol in Sacramento."

Mrs. Clark conveyed her husband's wish that his remains be buried on the Capitol grounds. The legislature promised to take the matter under consideration. It ended there.

Construction of the Capitol at an early stage.

Courtesy of the Sacramento Museum and History Department

CHAPTER XI

A Capitol of Its Own: The Completion
Gordon P. Cummings' Contribution

Clark's assistant, Gordon P. Cummings, was appointed Capitol Architect, January 2, 1866. Cummings had been trained in England and had worked on the Montgomery Block, a famous commercial development in San Francisco. He remained in charge until completion, except for an 18 month period in 1870 to 1872.

Cummings made major contributions to design and ornamentation of the building as well as overseeing execution. In his 1869 report to the Capitol Commissioners, he writes of preparing elaborate drawings for the grounds, dome, porticos, and steps.

Removal attempts run like a red thread through the story of the Capitol. In February 1866, Senator Thomas Hardy introduced a resolution to report on the advisability of donating the Capitol and all state owned buildings in Sacramento to the city. The new Capitol would be located "at some other locality." The Senate set the resolution aside.

Although Cummings seems to have been liberal and fairminded, he had periodic labor troubles. They must have been as irritating as a hair shirt. The stonecutters walked off the building in 1866. Cummings had fired one of the workers and the other men refused to work until he was reinstated. They charged Cummings was incompetent to supervise the stonecutting.

Cummings and the Capitol became involved in a minor scandal in October, when three cracks were discovered in the west wall. Facing the Sacramento River, it had been built up faster than the rest of the building for a "good show."

Work halted for an investigation. The U. S. Corp. of Engineers reported the cause to be uneven settling with no effect on the foundation. The problem remedied, it was said to be "more a blemish than a defect." The Capitol Commissioners exonerated Cummings. A careful watch revealed no further widening.

The Capitol Commissioners reconsidered the matter of materials in 1867. Granite was to be used only on the exterior walls of the first story. The granite came from state quarries, a gift of Central Pacific Railroad in return for financial assistance in building the transcontinental railroad. The lower course of granite, a dark gray, was quarried at Folsom by prisoners from newly established Folsom Prison. The lighter gray granite came from quarries near Rocklin.

The entire second story was completed in 1867 as well as almost one-third of the iron work. This included the ornamental iron work around windows and pilasters. "As castings", enthused the *Bee*, "they could not be excelled."

After several years of relative calm, agitation for removal surfaced again in 1868. It started with a resolution presented by Assemblyman Francis Giltner on January 10th, requesting examination of the Capitol's safety from flood damage, expenditures, cost of completion, and other matters. A modified resolution passed both houses.

The Capitol's west side during the original construction.   Photo from the California State Library, circa 1867

Original construction from the east, showing the semi-circular apse.   Photo from the Sacramento Museum and History Department

For several months removal bill followed removal bill. On January 23rd, Giltner introduced a bill for removal to San José. The city was to furnish a capitol free of charge for six years after which a state-erected building would be ready.

On January 30th, an Assembly bill preamble reiterated that the capitol would still cost several hundred thousand dollars, a heavy burden to tax payers. Moreover, "serious doubts exist in the minds of a large portion of the people....as to the safety of Sacramento from floods." It provided that whenever San Francisco, San José or Benicia would provide a suitable site and erect a Capitol to cost at least $400,000 for the State, all work on the Capitol would stop. That city would be declared the seat of government, and as soon as practical, State officers would move, along with archives and public property.

A similar bill in February renewed the argument as to whether or not San José was still the constitutional seat of government. It provided for a board of State officers, who would meet in San José and select a site for a Capitol. If San José erected a suitable building free of charge before October 1, 1869, the seat of government would be removed to that city.

On February 4th, the Dashaway Club, a temperance organization in Santa Cruz, offered use of its hall for 10 years as a State Capitol.

On February 7th, authorities of San José and Santa Clara County formally invited members of the legislature and their friends to take a free special train to San José. The City Council offered any public park as a site for a Capitol. The County Board of Supervisors renewed its offer of free use of its courthouse for five years.

The Senate succumbed to the free ride to San José. It also visited Oakland on the invitation of city officers. The Assembly declined.

The legislature could finally turn to other matters. One of the first bills considered provided for repeal of the special tax for construction of the Capitol.

All bills failed, but that failed to stop removal attempts in the future. Were the removal bills motivated by honest fear of Sacramento's floods or construction problems? Were they purely political?

The Committee on Capitol Buildings compiled a 100 page handwritten report with the opinions of many men. It concluded that flood damge threatened the Capitol.

However, Sacramento had not suffered from floods since the high grading of city streets. On Christmas Eve 1867, the city survived an acid test, when flood waters submerged lands to the north and east—but left Sacramento untouched.

Cummings favored giving the workmen some incentives to prevent increasing wages. Evidently, this did not please his troublesome employees. A group designated "high cockolorums" by the Bee visited Governor Haight and demanded Cummings' resignation. The governor refused to be influenced. The Bee applauded his position: "...to remove that officer now would be looked upon by thinking men as scarcely less than sacrilege."

Labor troubles, compounded by shortages of materials, continued. Workers struck in April, except for carpenters, blacksmiths and a few laborers. Brick production stopped.

When it resumed, work began on the outer dome, but that, too, was held up until iron arrived. The roofing program had to be delayed for arrival of the iron cornice.

In September, Cummings was cheered by some good news. His specifications and designs for white marble fireplaces were accepted—cost $5,000.

Work continued slowly through April 1869. The bricklayers, carpenters, plasterers, and laborers petitioned the Board for a raise. The Board granted a raise to the carpenters. The next day, all the mechanics refused to work unless they, too, received an increase. Cummings felt he had to promise raises or stop work. The laborers followed their example the day after.

At the end of September, the blacksmiths and painters asked for a raise. Cummings reported, "I had to increase carpenter's wages 25 cents a day or lose my best workers."

To quiet labor union dissatisfaction, the legislature reduced the work day on all state jobs from 10 to 8 hours.

The Capitol experienced momentous change in 1869. While much remained unfinished, interiors suggested future elegance, particularly in the legislative halls and East Apse.

The inner dome was complete. Workmen laid the last brick in the rotunda. Cast iron bearheads filled the medallions on the frieze in the upper rotunda. Gas fixtures were installed even though a man-ahead-of-his-times offered to light the Capitol with electricity.

Packets of gold leaf, Chinese vermillion, and rose-pink paint arrived to decorate the delicate carved moldings and plaster ornamentation.

Wagons and drays hauled the archives to their new home. Carpets arrived for the governor's office, new desks for the legislators, and such mundane necessities as stationery and brooms.

Two saloons, anticipating thirsty lawmakers, opened on nearby corners.

On November 25th, gas lights illuminated the Senate and Assembly for the first time. The contractor uncorked champagne; workers raised their glasses in toasts to the occasion.

The 1869 Legislature—the first to occupy the Capitol—on the west steps.   *Photo from the Sacramento Museum and History Department*

The roof was on and state officers were overeager to move to their new quarters. Governor Henry Haight moved into three rooms on the southwest corner, November 26th. Secretary of State Nichols moved the same day.

The Supreme Court met for the first time in the East Apse, a semicircular wing, December 3rd. An iron railing, painted gold bronze, surrounded the space assigned to the bar. The judge's bench was white with panels of laurel wood.

The first case was scarcely dignified. Nellie Smith and Anna Keating, two saloon girls, were accused of violating an ordinance prohibiting women from exhibiting themselves in a saloon after midnight. They lost their case and went to jail.

Three days later, the legislature held its first session in its new quarters—the same location as today. The Senate occupied the southeast corner. The Assembly occupied the northeast corner. Massive doors to both chambers were made of black walnut, paneled in laurel, with scrollwork detailing. There were 20 windows in the Senate and 22 in the Assembly covered with folding blinds. All were of glass imported from Belgium and shipped around the

Horn. There were two gasoliers (chandeliers lit by gas) in the Senate, and three in the Assembly, each with 64 clusters of lights.

Corinthian columns supported public galleries that extended across the back and around the side walls. On opening day, the many ladies in galleries gushed over the wildflowers painted on the assembly ceiling. They thought the statue of Minerva, above the dais in the Senate, "most impressive."

A few days later, Emperor Norton I appeared in his customary navy blue general's uniform, lavish with gold braid and heavily fringed epaulets. A tall beaver hat with cockade of feathers topped his curly brown hair. The well known San Francisco character, whose legal name was Joshua Norton, had operated a highly successful real estate concern. He failed in his attempt to corner the rice market, losing his entire fortune and the investments of his friends. Unable to cope with financial disaster, he had discarded reality for the role of Emperor Norton, ruler of the United States and Mexico. Although, he praised the Capitol royally, the Emperor was "grieved" by Sacramento's dirty streets and ordered them cleaned up.

Norton visited the legislature often, for he considered observing the lawmakers one of the duties of his rule. When Norton attended San Francisco Council meetings, he always took along his constant companions, mongrel dogs Bummer and Lazarus. Undoubtedly, they accompanied him to the Capitol.

The Grand Capitol Ball, December 15th, sponsored by Sacramento citizens, christened the chambers of both houses. Several hundred of the most prominent people, legislators, and state officials attended. Carriages drew up before the brilliantly illuminated building. Out stepped ladies, glittering with jewels, elegant in gowns of silk, satin, moiré, and uncut velvet. The gentlemen rivaled the women in elegance: dress coats lined with white satin, somber vests, polished boots, tight black pantaloons, white neckties. Some of the men, not so fashionably dressed, were excused as being "country members."

Flower-bedecked tables, accommodating 500 at a time lined the corridors. Hundreds of gaslights lent magnificence to the chamber/ballrooms. Guests danced sedate quadrilles in the Senate; "fancy dances of the day" in the Assembly. The menu, printed in French, featured "luxuries and substantials." The long list included lobster a la mayonaise, pigs a la Californienne, snipes a la Malakoff, and venison a la Americaine. After the midnight supper, guests "tripped the light fantastic until hours of the early morning."

While government went on inside, construction continued on the outside. The lawmakers entered by ramp. The basement, the balustrade, the pediment, the attic, the outside dome were still unfinished. Scaffolding enfolded the entire building.

Some $700,000 had been spent. "In my opinion," said Cummings, "another $40,000 to $50,000 is needed to finish the buildings and grounds."

With the move, the legislature decided it wanted the Capitol finished in short order. It approved 15 year bonds in the amount of $250,000 on April 4, 1870. The appropriation included $50,000 for a governor's mansion that was begun, but never finished.

The Board of Capitol Commissioners released Cummings from his position on August 26, 1870, and sent

Hauling the cast iron columns through Sacramento to the Capitol site. The columns were 30 feet long, four feet in diameter with four inch thick cast iron walls. Each weighed 11½ tons, and were used for the porticos and colonnade.
Photo from F. Hal Higgins Library of Agricultural Technology, University of California at Davis, 1871

him on a trip to the East to buy materials for the Capitol. His ability was unquestioned. The new administration favored friends and chose A. A. Bennett, of Kennitzer and Bennett, as Capitol Architect.

In their report to the Commissioners, October 1871, the new architects found fault with their predecessor. They charged Cummings had failed to follow plans, changing the original octagon dome to circular and the Roman architectural details to Grecian style. They planned, also, to omit the granite steps in front, calling them "heavy, costly, and useless."

The grand granite stairs to the second story had focused attention on the legislative branch of the government. Building the stairs to the first story changed the focus of the Capitol building to the executive offices.

The delivery of the columns for the porticos caused enormous interest. The columns were monolithic— 30 feet in length, 4 feet in diameter, 4 inches thick and weighted 11 1/2 tons. The columns were unloaded at the wharf and hauled in large wagons. To expedite delivery, a steam tractor was shipped from San Francisco. A huge derrick aided by fifteen men raised the columns into position on the portico. They were painted white to simulate stone and filled with coke to prevent condensation and rusting of interior surfaces.

It was the newcomer, A. A. Bennett, who crowned the dome with the gold gilded ball, a fitting occasion for celebration. He invited state officials and members of the press to witness the ceremony. At 2 p.m. sharp, on October 30, 1871, "boxes" that were to elevate them to the dome began what must have been a shaky ascent.

The 60 pound copper ball, gilded with $300 in smelted gold coin, hung in the dome framework, covered with a sheet. At a signal from Bennett, the foreman raised the ball in place. Secretary of State, Dr. Nichols, unveiled the ball with appropriate words, "Our fair State—may its bright name and reputation forever remain as bright and untarnished as this golden ball."

From the pinnacle 212 feet above the earth the company looked out over Sacramento. On the east, the mighty Sierra Nevada; on the west the Coast Range; on the north, snow-capped Mt. Shasta; and on the south, Mt. Diablo. They could see the course of the Sacramento and American Rivers and their confluence as one great river.

In an exuberant mood, heightened by plentiful champagne, "they toasted all and everything to be thought of up there." As a final gesture, the officials and workmen scratched their names on the redwood pedestal: Dr. H. L. Nichols (Secretary of State), A. F. Cornell with a rubric (State Treasurer), Robert Watt (State Controller), A. A. Bennett (Architect), and eight others (the contractor and craftsmen). The names were still clear when the weathered pedestal was taken down in 1953.

When Bennett failed to complete the Capitol satisfactorily, the Commissioners called Cummings back from the East. He must have felt a glow of satisfaction as he resumed his former position, May 1872.

On reappointment, Cummings was occupied with "completion projects." He strengthened the foundation at its weakest points, corrected the "very bad state of steam and water pipes," improved rotunda walls, arched the floor for tiles, finished the copper roof of the portico, and made progress in general.

Cummings recommended the rotunda be repainted, the color to be a "tint of fresco with gold points as near white as possible." He thought the present color of "brickdust and Scotch snuff" cast a pall of gloom over everything. The rotunda wood floor was only a temporary arrangement. According to Cummings in August 1872, "The rotunda floor has been removed— none too soon, as the thin walls were crumbling, and would have fallen, with all the gas and water pipes attached to them."

He also laid English encaustic tile in a geometric pattern in the upper rotunda, laid marble tile in the hall, and encircled the upper rotunda well with a handsome walnut railing.

Cummings approached the task of securing sculpture to the triangular pediment (tympanum) happily. Peter Mazzara, well-known San Francisco sculptor, made the figures in clay, then had them cast in ground stone. The central figure, helmeted and holding a lance, was Minerva, Goddess of Wisdom. The other allegorical figures: Education, holding tablet and globe; Industry, leaning on an anchor and plough; Justice, holding a tablet; and Mining, leaning on a pick and hammer.

The architect frequently disagreed with Mazzara. This time he enthused, "It's one of the finest pieces of statuary and our chances of getting a better, or even one as good are small."

The sculptures were secured to the pediment before funds ran out in January 1873 and work stopped until August.

The Capitol Commissioners' report for 1873 stated Cummings had "discharged his duties faithfully and ably."

Cummings complimented the Commissioners on the substitution of "Ransome," a cast stone, for the balustrade, instead of using iron. "It was beautiful, cheaper, and needed no maintenance."

The report also summarized recent accomplishments. A large portion of the money had been used to bring the grounds "into their present beautiful condition."

Attention had turned to the grounds in 1871-72.

Completed Capitol with picket fence. The fence was made from leftover scaffolding.   *Photo from the California State Library, 1879*

Eight hundred tiny saplings had been planted in soil enriched with silt. The Agricultural Society could take credit for the 200 varieties. Organized in 1854, they corresponded with horticultural societies all over the world.

A neat white picket fence made from salvaged scaffolding, surrounded the grounds. Although incongruous with the classic revival architecture, it kept out wandering cows and horses. Plank sidewalks protected the solon's boots from summer dust and winter mud.

Capitol grounds expanded by five blocks between L and N and Twelfth and Fifteenth in 1872. Capitol Commissioners had condemned the property. Its appraisal of $142,423.40 exceeded the $100,000 appropriation for its purchase. Community-minded Sacramentans came forward with money to make up the difference. Later the city voted a special tax of 20 cents on $100 to be used to reimburse the citizens who had advanced the money.

Undoubtedly, Bennett's niggling criticism of Cum-

ming's work still rankled, for he couldn't resist taking his turn at criticism. He appended his comments to the Commissioner's report. In his words, but shortened: "The original lead roof gutters have been changed without much improvement. The four flights of very elegant stairs are uselessly expensive. The front of the Capitol has received two coats of paint, but the balance is only whitewashed. Two useless columns have been added to the Supreme Court, and a *preposterous* flagpole to the grounds."

"The system of steam heat that replaced mine is of faulty construction, difficult to maintain, and expensive. (Its boilers used 2 1/2 cords of wood a day.) What is wanted is copious drafts of atmospheric air, regulated in each chamber."

Cummings reserved his most vituperative criticism for the dome's crown. "The little round top with the gilt ball is simply ridiculous." He wanted a bronze figure, at least six feet high at the apex. "If not done, whatever may be the beauties of the building and grounds, the defect will forever remain a slur on our taste."

Perhaps, he changed his mind later, for he called the building, "the most perfect combination of stone, iron, brick, and mortar I have ever seen and seems intended to last all time and ages."

In addition to the statues for the pediment, the Commissioners engaged Mazzara to create sculptures to be placed at the north, south and west porticos. At each corner, eleven or twelve foot high statues would represent "War", "Peace", "Prudence", and "Force". In between were to be statues seven feet high of "Fame", "Eloquence", and "Verity". Fourteen richly ornamented vases 3 1/2' to 5 1/2' would complete the grouping. The total cost including placing was to be $34,500.

With the statuary on the parapet walls in place, all that remained to be finished in 1873 were exterior details. Cummings drew up plans for a fence to replace the temporary pickets. Of cast iron and granite, it was not just a fence. It was exciting in concept, the granite posts ornamented with grizzly bear heads, terminated in acorn tops.

He also drew plans for contoured cast iron stairs to fit the terraced grounds. Lamp posts at the bottom of the stairs and large vases with flowering plants completed a design to truly complement the Capitol. The official report for 1874-75 gave the total cost as $2,449,429.31.

When was the capitol completed?

The event slipped by unnoticed. Later, nobody knew the answer.

Archivist Dr. J. N. Bowman did some research. He concluded it was the date of Architect Cummings last paycheck, February 8, 1874.

At last, at least in print, the customary three cheers of that day!

Three cheers for Reuben Clark, who put so much of himself into the Capitol. Three cheers for A. A. Bennett, who topped the dome with a gold gilded ball. Three cheers for Gordon P. Cummings, who completed the Capitol.

Three cheers for the Capitol of California!

Photo from the California Department of Parks and Recreation

Capitol and grounds.

Photo from the California State Library, circa 1888

Rotunda with statue of Isabella and Columbus. The two eyepieces of the stereoscope gave a three dimensional effect to the card. Popular parlor entertainment at the turn-of-the-century.   Photo from State Capitol Museum Collection, a stereocard, circa 1900

CHAPTER XII
The Great Remodeling

Completion had little meaning for the Capitol. Architect-historian Raymond Girvigian notes, "Constant change was in reality the only permanent condition of the Capitol up to the present time. Work never reached full conclusion before something else was done."

A sorely needed paint job left the Capitol a glistening white in 1877. Sides and back must have been washed free of whitewash by then. The front had been painted before.

The following year artificial stone replaced the gravel walks and planked driveway.

The years 1880 to the turn of the century were relatively quiet years for both California and the Capitol, with only minor additions, repairs, and improvements. Soon enough, the Great Remodeling of 1906 would completely change the character of the Capitol.

A driveway for carriages and exercising horses was placed in the center of Capitol Park. Today its location is still visible, marked by an oval of English elms.

Old photos show the trees in the park planted in stiff rows as straight as soldiers lined up for inspection. An 1880 planting of native trees used the "French system" of natural grouping. Also the upper cupola dome of the building was gilded. Efforts to have the entire dome gilded failed. Gold leaf was too expensive.

Architect Cummings' plans for an ornate classic cast iron and granite fence were to reach fruition. The first 16 ton granite blocks arrived from the Rocklin quarries. Folsom prison furnished granite "of the finest quality" for the base. The fence, with its massive gate posts, was finished in 1883. Without the entrance gate posts, cost ran $10 per lineal foot.

The statue of Columbus at the Court of Spain was set on a foot high base of polished granite in the rotunda with proper ceremony, on December 22, 1883. Larkin Goldsmith Meade, an American in Florence, Italy, had sculptured the eight foot high figures out of a single block of unflawed marble from the Greek Islands.

Isabella of Spain, seated on her throne, lifts a fabulous pearl necklace in a pledge to finance the explorer's expeditions. Columbus kneels at her left; on her right is a richly dressed page.

Darius Ogden Mills, pioneer Sacramento banker, purchased the sculpture from the original owner for $30,000 and presented it to the state. "Soap and water once a year keep it glistening white," according to the 1958 *Blue Book*.

Governor Waterman felt strongly enough about the condition of the basement to comment on it in his message of 1889. "...that the basement was in a filthy condition would but meagerly describe it." The basement was "thoroughly cleansed, fumigated, and whitewashed."

Originally, the basement was dank and dark without windows or doors. Over the years it served as a dumping ground for building debris, ashes, old paper and other rubbish. The figures can scarcely be believed, but Archivist J. N. Bowman reports removal of 800 to 1000 tons of refuse. The trash was scattered throughout the grounds to fill low areas.

E. G. Waite took office as Secretary of State January, 1891. Energetic, stubborn, and persistent, he determined to solve the maintenance problems that had outwitted his predecessors. He had a discouraging beginning: an overdrawn budget and long list of problems.

Cesspool problems, before modern plumbing, were a fact of life. The Capitol was no exception. The cesspool had not been cleaned for years. Waite had the pipes flushed and the openings, which allowed sewer gas to escape, closed. Some pipes were rotten and needed to be replaced. Plans for the building had no indication of plumbing. A former boy apprentice plumber testified, "The contractors received pay by the pound and the more they could bury in the walls the fatter the job." Some large lead pipes went nowhere.

Waite needed a plan of the gas pipes before he could install electrical wiring, running through the same pipes. To obtain the plan, he hired a former employee familiar with the layout.

That taken care of, Waite dealt with the long-standing chimney problem. For years, coal smoke, soot, and cinders had filled "all but the governor's office" on stormy days. "The problem couldn't be solved," according to everyone. Waite heightened the chimneys and apparently did away with the problem. There were no more complaints.

Waite wrestled with the roof next. Painted canvas patches were fastened with nails. Holes and leaks developed wherever nails came into contact with the copper roof. Waite hired the roofer of 20 years ago to remove the patches and repair the roof. Results were apparently satisfactory.

A storm of "huge magnitude" hit Sacramento November 1892. Waite, summoned to the Capitol, found water pouring into the chambers. Several employees and Waite, himself, ascended the roof with timbers which they nailed down. The biggest leaks were stopped with putty, saving the south wing from damage.

Waite wrote a friend:

> They say I would have made a good subject for a caricature during the late storm. The copper roof rose and fell in waves, broke loose, and streams came through, threatening destruction of thousands of dollars worth of frescos. I went on that roof when the wind blew a hurricane, and had timbers spiked down upon it. My hat took a notion to navigate the air and left me. I thought the feathers would all be blown off me. But the work was done, the holes puttied up, and the property saved. But I did think my clothes would whip me to death, or that I would be blown to Marysville without any stopover

privileges. Those brave fellows under my command braved the pitiless wind and rain and did work for the state when skilled roofers declined the job for coin.

He had the roof repaired properly after the storm. "No hurricane can ever disturb it," he stated optimistically, "and I am pleased to report that the roof leaks no more."

To Waite, also, fell the job of completing the fireproof, moistureproof, and burglarproof vault in the basement for the state archives.

The account of the earthquake, April 21, 1892, appeared under the headline, "THE CAPITOL SUFFERS". A statuette on the portico fell to earth 40 feet from the building. (Years later restoration workers still found plaster shards in the lawn.) A ceiling crack extended from one end of the building to the other, with the Assembly ceiling of stucco tipped with gold receiving the greatest damage.

Electricity generated excitement in 1892. A carload or more of chandeliers and gas fixtures were taken down and sent to San Francisco to be electri-

Senate Chamber before remodeling—George Washington portrait watches the Senate.

Photo from the California State Library Collection, circa 1890

Senate Chamber before remodeling.

fied. People remained a mite skeptical of new-fangled electricity. The lower lights of the chandeliers were wired for electricity, the upper lights were left to burn gas, in case of a failure. There were to be 1,400 incandescent lights in the building, "with wires to be arranged for five hundred additional, should they be required in the future."

The total cost was $16,000; $9,000 for electrifying and rewiring; $7,000 for rebronzing and new fixtures. The "electrified" Capitol opened for public inspection New Year's Eve.

Waite was particularly pleased by the change to incandescent light, for he considered it healthier than gas. He had long been a critic of the Capitol's lack of proper ventilation. "Healthy air makes the healthy blood that makes healthy brains. Bad air induces bad legislation."

He justified the installation with these figures: Each gas jet burned seven feet of oxygen an hour and there were 227 in the Assembly alone. He concluded: "The substitution of incandescent electric lamps for gas lights in the chamber is the equivalent of the removal of more than 2,700 men" in its effect on a healthy atmosphere.

Years of soot had dulled the Library's walls and ceilings. Waite decided to redecorate while the library was still torn up from electrification. A *Bee* reporter described the results in glowing terms. It featured a monochromatic color scheme of "ivory yellow" and delicate brown. Ceilings were frescoed, with designs in plaster of open books and a globe. The Corinthian columns, painted the same "ivory yellow" looked "very majestic." Stained glass topped the dome and "in the morning, when the sun is back of the Capitol, the effect of the glowing colors on the interior of the library is exquisite and beautiful."

The capitol's demands for attention were as impossible to satisfy as those of a nagging wife—or husband. The legislature appropriated $25,000 for repairs, carpets and elevator in 1893. The Capitol was painted gleaming white except for the dome roof. It was painted green-gray to imitate slate with glossy white ribs.

Redecoration of the Judges chambers touched off a small decorating spree. "The ceilings yawned continually with unsightly cracks." Frescoes not only cured the "yawns" but were works of art, described as depicting cornstalks, leaves, cobs and tassels. They were hand painted in tones of cream, salmon, and turquoise with raised effect in gold and aluminum leaf.

The Constitution of 1879 provided for removal after approval by two-thirds of the legislature and ratification by the majority of the voters at a special election. Supposedly, the provision made it impossible to transfer the capital.

In 1893, the legislature was comfortably ensconced in a state-owned building, set in landscaped grounds. Amazingly, new efforts for removal surfaced once again.

In March 11, 1893, Senate Constitutional Amendment No. 23, to be submitted to the people, proposed San José be declared the seat of government. Certain conditions were to be met: donation of an approved site of not less than ten acres and one million dollars to be paid to the State Treasury. The amendment was adopted in the Senate 27-8; in the Assembly 57-7. A motion to reconsider was laid on the table on the 13th.

The proposal alarmed Sacramento. Elated San Joseans prepared to raise funds. The Supreme Court hastened to put forth their opinion that the action for removal was invalid.

The stormy 1893 session was beset with scandal. The *Sacramento Bee* muttered in print, "Thank God, the Legislature is about to adjourn!" The upset legislators vented their outraged feelings in the removal effort.

The scandal had to do with the sale of liquor in the Capitol. Legislators patronized "The Well", a saloon/restaurant in the basement, to such an extent that it interfered with legislation. The bar was ordered closed, but liquor sales continued at the tables.

In 1893, Assemblyman A. J. Bledsoe of Eureka, took on "The Well" as a personal crusade. He asked that a five-man committee be created to investigate. He questioned, "By what right or authority does the legal custodian of the State Capitol allow a saloon and restaurant to be maintained in the basement?" (Sale of liquor at the Capitol had been prohibited in 1850.)

The matter was referred to the Committee of Public Morals with Bledsoe as chairman. Bledsoe pursued the matter, but the Democratic majority desired that the saloon be maintained.

One legislator claimed he had been entirely ignorant of "The Well," and that Bledsoe's campaign was a boon to business.

Certainly everyone was aware of "The Well" after two stories with graphic descriptions and illustrations by the *Bee's* artist ran in 1893. The articles wrote euphemistically of "ladies of Eve" and "ladies of the half-world" who clinked glasses with the legislators. Chris Buckley, political boss, who had made "many and many a dollar" during the legislative session, invited the "most shapely women and set-up

The 1900 Assembly in session.

champagne" the last night. Soon "The Well" was the scene of the can-can and indecencies over which "the curtain had better be drawn."

"The Well" was intended as a place for temperance drinks and lunch but "the barkeeper was busier than the cook." Its partitions and dark corners gave a certain amount of privacy. Lobbyists intent on a deal or purchase of a vote found it a convenience. Also, it served as a hideaway for legislators who wanted to dodge roll call.

Despite the scandal during his four year tenure, Waite's efforts received a good evaluation. A newspaper article praised him as the only Secretary of State who gave more than a "lick and promise" to the Capitol and termed the results as "showing handsome returns for his outlay."

Waite died in office in 1894. Despite his improvements and attention to detail, his successor, Secretary of State L. H. Brown, found much to criticize. The flooring in parts of the building needed replacement badly. The worn cocoa matting covering the third floor corridors had been patched with oilcloth. The legislature approved the expenditure May 26, 1895. Evidently, Brown was economy-minded for he replaced the matting with linoleum taken up from the first floor when tile had been installed.

Brown was also concerned about the lack of a fire protection system. In the opinion of the Chief Engineer of the Sacramento Fire Department, "A fire starting in the attic would quickly destroy the entire building." Fire extinguishers were placed in corridors and offices for at least some measure of protection.

Secretary of State C. F. Curry shared Brown's anxiety about fire. A fire drill demonstrated that water could not be sprayed above the Capitol's second story. Curry reported, "In case of fire, we are at the mercy of one little hydrant that only gives a one and one-half inch flow of water." Curry wrote an emphatic letter to the mayor requesting a larger connection. In 1902, the matter went to the Sacramento Grand Jury for an investigation.

He, also, ordered the attic cleaned out "by removing a large amount of lumber, furniture, and rubbish, all of which has been saved up and used for kindling."

Turn-of-the-century, the phrase suggests new beginnings. Change was in the air and the Capitol was not immune. The early 1900's brought drastic changes. Governor Pardee gave forwarning in his biennial message, January 5, 1905. He stated: "Although the Capitol was a noble building, and a great credit to earlier generations of California...in its plumbing and heating systems it is sadly antiquated, besides being out of repair in a good many ways....Little has been done in the last 3-5 years to

replace the primitive conveniences with more modern ones."

The changes to the interior became known as the "Great Remodeling of 1906." The work was authorized. Architects Sutton and Weeks drew plans. Contracts for the extensive remodeling, repairing, and completion of the attic and basement were signed on April 13, 1906.

Five days later, April 18, 1906, an earthquake, an estimated 8.3 on the Richter scale, cut a swath of destruction 50 miles wide and 300 miles long. For San Francisco, it was a double diaster of earthquake and fire.

Fortunately, the State had signed $300,000 in bids, before demand for building materials had increased costs. Still, destruction of San Francisco foundries made fabrication of iron work difficult and delayed orders for materials.

By May, progress was being made on the new elevator at the north end. A newspaper article mentioned that the elevator would be used to lower the statues on the parapets before they fell down. The earthquake made everyone apprehensive.

The extensive remodeling meant inconvenience. Library materials—books, newspaper files, and maps—had to be placed in storage. The Assembly moved to the Redman's Hall. The Senate met in Turn Verein Hall. Executive offices remained at the Capitol even though officials suffered from cold feet while the heating system was repaired.

Complaints about the foul air and noxious odors raged practically from first moving to the building. Perhaps the new ventilating system would solve the problem. It included a chamber in the attic with "fans and other devices for drawing foul air from all rooms and supplying fresh pure air." Workmen cut 40 windows in the basement, formerly "dark as a dungeon," so it could be used for storage and installation of machinery. Their compressed air drills had difficulty in getting through the nearly "hard-as-granite" brick.

The contractor, Mr. Campbell, warned that the roof trusses of 12" x 14" pine had dry rot: "The beams are a menace in danger of collapse." They were replaced with steel.

He gave his professional opinion, "In all else the structure is sound and a marvel of solidity, strength, and fine workmanship."

The most drastic remodeling was reserved for the Senate and Assembly chambers. Photos appearing in the *Sacramento Union* showed virtually total devastation. The short caption explained. "The ceilings of both chambers, the paintings and ornaments were removed, and the present roof is the blue vault of heaven. Brick and lumber litter the floor."

The demolition prepared for lower ceilings in order

Construction work on the Capitol.   *Photo from the Sacramento Museum and History Department, circa 1906 (Harold Simmonds Collection)*

to add a fourth floor. Workmen placed ten-ton steel trusses on the roof over the Legislative Chambers— four over the Senate, three over the Assembly. After each truss was cut in sections, workmen lifted them by hand.

The graceful fluted Corinthian columns and pilasters were removed. The massive round columns that replaced them were painted to resemble marble "with admirable accuracy." A five foot lincrusta border was painted red in the Senate and green in the Assembly.

The drapes on lower windows were of rich plush with bunches of California poppies woven into the fabric. The ecru net curtains featured a grizzly bear center with poppies on the four borders. Floors were covered with carpet in a "unique design." The side galleries were omitted.

The members black walnut desks with leather inset and the handcarved daises remained the same. Many of the architectural details had been removed, the richly colored ceiling banished by white paint. The new appearance was stark and cold.

Governor Pardee's office boasted hand-carved black walnut furniture. A unique feature, it was said, was the "California poppy and cloud and sky effects on the ceiling and frieze of the walls, which are tinted a delicate green with a five-foot wainscot of pure white lincrusta decorated with gold leaf scrolls...."

No two of the state offices were decorated alike. The ceilings and friezes were painted with motifs of flowers, scrollwork touched with gold, or the seal of the state.

By late 1907, alterations were nearly completed except for the legislative chambers. The grand walnut staircases with carved bear heads on the newel posts had been torn out and replaced with a fire-proof ones of wrought iron and marble. The interior dome had been painted for artistic effect. Scroll and figure work decorated wall panels in the rotunda. Heating, lighting, ventilating, and plumbing systems had been replaced. Mantels were removed from the 55 original fireplaces.

The state held auctions to dispose of the surplus

furniture, building materials, and mantels. The carved, solid marble mantels brought $1.00 each.

Remodeling cost $377,925, bringing the cost of the Capitol to $2,972,985.

This time the removal bill was introduced in the very midst of Great Remodeling on February 21, 1907. G. R. Lukens introduced the Senate bill to change the Capitol to Berkeley.

Cartoonists found the subject choice material for the newspapers. It was also, amazingly, considered seriously by the majority of the legislators.

One Senator jokingly submitted a solution to the perennial problem: "Resolved that there is hereby appropriated out of the State Treasury the sum of $200,000 for the purpose of buying a large automobile on which may be placed the state Capitol thus hauling it about the state to suit the whim of disgruntled politicians and real estate boomers."

The Committee on Public Buildings and Grounds recommended a "do pass." After lengthy debate, the bill passed the Senate 30-9, and the Assembly 59-18. Governor Gillett approved the bill March 6, 1907.

Citizens voted in the November, 1908 general election, on removal of the seat of government to the town of Berkeley on January 1, 1909. It was defeated by a two to one margin. (87,378 ayes 165,630 noes)

The chief complaint about the remodeling seems entirely warranted. The elevators, installed during the remodeling, were slow and frequently inoperative. The Capitol Superintendent leaked the information that the equipment was secondhand. The elevators, survivors of the San Francisco fire and earthquake, had been salvaged from the Monadock Building and sold to the state.

Not all opinions on the remodeling were favorable. Some legislators agreed with Senator Caminetti that the Capitol had been "architecturally butchered."

Portion of the State Library which was in the apse until 1928.   *Photo from the California State Library, circa 1904*

CHAPTER XIII
The State Outgrows the Capitol

A few years of relief came, after the hectic upheaval and remodeling. Yet, at this period, the first ideas of expansion burgeoned, a forewarning of what was to come.

The modern phase of California's economic history dates from 1910-1915 with the opening of the Panama Canal, the automotive age, the development of oil, the growth of irrigated agriculture, the beginnings of the movie industry, the large-scale manufacturing.

Governor James Gillett complained of the inconvenience caused by crowded conditions. He stated his conviction, "The state has outgrown the Capitol. The State Library alone takes up half of the top floor ... and a great portion of the first, second, and third floors."

The Library ranked second among state libraries for its reference collection. It also circulated four sets of traveling libraries to communities to generate interest in starting their own libraries. From 1914 to 1920 it sponsored a library school atop the apse. Old photos show the students sitting at plain desks, dressed almost alike in middies and skirts with long hair in buns.

Originally, all state offices had been housed in the Capitol. Although prohibited by law, by 1912 fully one third of the offices had moved to San Francisco.

In October 1912, the Special Commission recommended the acquisition of two blocks of land, facing the Capitol, for erection of a State Library and Courts Building and a State Office Building. They also recommended that Sacramento adopt a bond issue to help pay for the land. Their report concluded: Space needed was 153 rooms; space available in the Capitol was 99 rooms.

Sacramento held a meeting to put the matter of the purchase of two additional blocks between Ninth and Tenth and L and N before its citizens. They voted at a special election to bond the city for $700,000 for land purchase. The matter was urgent. It was rumored San Francisco had offered Civic Center property, if the State would appropriate $1,000,000 for the erection of an Annex.

The legislature appropriated money through a $3 million bond issue November, 1914. Construction had to be postponed due to wartime conditions. Meanwhile, costs of materials and labor escalated, forcing Governor Stephens to request increased appropriations. A Supreme Court ruling (1926) made the Extension Buildings a legal part of the Capitol. Only a short distance away, the new buildings fronted a circle of lawn, flowers, and fountain. Of classic design, the buildings' exteriors were mirror images, with pediments and statues reposing on each side of the entrance stairs.

The buildings, completed in June, 1928, cost $5,400,000. Immediately, government offices began a game of musical chairs. The Controller and the Purchasing Department moved in as the State Library moved out. The Controller occupied the first three floors of the apse. Since the office issues warrants for

Pediment of the State Library and courts building.   *Photo by Leonard McKay*

all state expenditures, its need for greater space reflected the government's expansion.

Sadly, although reference materials were as good in the new library and courts building, it lacked the ambience that charmed everyone who used the library in the Apse.

During this time, the lively aspect of the Capitol Rotunda changed when the niches were covered with murals. The legislature awarded a $10,000 commission to Arthur F. Mathews, a much admired painter of that day.

Four groups of three panels each depicted phases of California's history in an allegorical manner. The first mural group portrayed the discovery of California and the coming of the "White Gods." The second of the three panels covers the Spanish-Mexican period. The third group portrayed the development of California. The fourth group showed the civilizing of the state with the last panel entitled "The Dream City of Beauty and Justice."

They were placed in the rotunda in time for the Panama Pacific International Exposition. The Mathews murals, painted in somber tones, were considered a landmark in California art.

The 1930's forced the Capitol to deal with the Great Depression and new technology.

While California suffered less than the rest of the nation from the depression, the affect on those who were unemployed was undoubtedly just as traumatic. In 1934, one fifth of the state's population was on relief—1,250,000 people.

Growth slowed during the 30's to its lowest level since 1850. Yet, California was a magnet for Arkies, for Oakies, and for Blacks from the deep South who hoped to find a better life or, at least, a better climate. The legislature passed an unenforceable and unconstitutional measure that closed state borders to "undesirables." Problems meant multiplying government.

Relief agencies had to find room in the Capitol. The sensible solution was to build mezzanines by slicing the high ceilinged rooms in half. And that is the way it was done. Photos of the period show one-half of a lovely arched window in one room. The bottom was on the floor below.

There was no time, patience or money for frills. The hand-painted dome ceiling, so delicately and beautifully colored, disappeared under a coat of practical green paint.

Razing the apse to build the East Annex.   *Photo from the California State Library, circa 1949*

The Governor's suite, also succumbed to space needs. Behind the previous alteration, the dismantling crew discovered an original ceiling, hand-painted with native wild flowers and the state seal. Remodeling gave Governor Culbert Olson a modern air conditioned private office. The new mezzanine addition, divided into a number of cubbyhole offices.

The war years, 1941-44, came hard on the heels of the Great Depression. Government offices had been straining at the seams; now they were bursting. Involvement in World War II generated such growth that it can be compared to that of the gold rush of a century before. From 1940 to 1950, population increased by 53.3 percent (6,907,387 to 10,586,223). For a six year period, California gained 1,315 residents each and every day.

All plans for expansion had to be delayed while dealing with the emergency of national survival. As the war drew to a close, the legislature appropriated $1,900,000 for what came to be called the East Annex as a solution to space problems.

State Architect Anson Boyd's first drawings, with the East Annex built around a central court, would have saved the East Apse. Pressure for greater space resulted in shelving the design.

The beautiful, beloved East Apse, once home of the State Library, was sacrificed.

Wrecking crews found the going tough. Walls were seven feet thick. Floors were supported by brick arches. Over a million bricks were salvaged, along with 40 to 50 tons of hand-forged beams. The intricately inlaid oak floors, the ornate ceilings, the spiraling iron stairs, the fluted columns—all became salvage.

The East Annex was in so-called "modified classic style" to blend in with the old Capitol. Senator James R. Mills, less diplomatic than honest, termed it "early prison architecture."

The East Annex was as different from the Capitol as a poster is from an oil painting. The skeleton of the Annex was concrete and steel. Its architectural features were composed of acoustical tile, flourescent lighting, plastic padding, aluminum frames. Luxury touches included the traditional marble lining the corridor walls and framing the 58 cases for county exhibits. Aluminum plaques by O. C. Malmquist decorated the main east entrance. The building was pronounced complete at a cost of $7,461,456.

The East Annex, completed in 1951 was described by Senator James Mills as "early prison architecture."

Photo by Leonard McKay

The best term for the Annex might be "functional." Its six stories cover eight acres of offices for the Governor, for the Senators and Assemblymen, and for other state officials.

On moving day late in 1951, Governor Warren felt a pang of regret at leaving the office that had housed California's governors for 82 years. At the last moment, he decided to take along his famous cork desk made by San Quentin prisoners and the grandfather clock that had occupied the outer office for years. On his way to the new annex office, he said, "I would rather be in the old building, if it had room for my staff."

The new office was jam-packed with the latest equipment: protection against wire-tapping, movie projector and screen, and even a private shower and dressing room. A streamlined desk and chairs complemented the ultra-modern private office.

From then on, the East Annex and the Old West Wing functioned as one unit, the Capitol.

Soon once again, spiraling growth would make space problems critical, further complicated by the need for earthquake safety. The fate of the Capitol would hang in precarious balance between legislators in favor of a new building and legislators in favor of preservation. Fortunately, the choice was made for restoration.

Architect Gordon Cummings statement on the completion of the Capitol in 1874 is still applicable. "It is the most perfect combination of stone, iron, brick and mortar I have ever seen and seems intended to last all time and ages."

Although inspired by classic tradition, the Capitol is distinctly Californian in character. Throughout themes from the Great Seal echo and re-echo, symbolic of the state's unique history and resources. The Capitol stands—a link to the past, a beacon for the future, and a source of pride for all Californians.

Bibliography

Bancroft, Hubert Howe. *History of California.* Vol. V-VI. San Francisco: The History Company, 1888.

Bean, Walton. *California, an Interpretative History.* New York: McGraw Hill, 1968.

Beilharz, Edwin A. and Donald O. DeMers, Jr. *San Jose.* Tulsa: Continental Heritage Press, 1980.

Biggs, Donald C. *Conquer and Colonize.* San Rafael: Presidio Press, 1977.

Bowman, J. N. "The Gold Ball of the Capitol Building." Bancroft Library. Berkeley, California. (typed.)

_____. "The Migrations of the California Capital." Master's thesis, University of California, Berkeley.

_____. Miscellaneous unpublished notes, Bancroft Library, Berkeley, California.

Browne, J. Ross. *The Debates of California on the Formation of the Constitution in September and October, 1849.* New York: Arno Press, 1850, 1973.

Bruce, John. *Gaudy Century.* New York: Random House, 1948.

Burnett, Peter. *An Old California Pioneer: Peter Burnett, First Governor of California.* Ward Ritchie, 1946.

California Blue Book (or State Roster). Compiled by the Secretary of State. Sacramento State Printing Office. 1903, 1907, 1909, 1942, 1958.

California. Department of Parks and Recreation. *Benicia Capitol State Historic Park.* (Leaflet).

California. Division of Architecture. *Capitol of California, 1853.* (Leaflet).

California. Journals of the Legislature, 1850, 1851, 1852, 1853, 1854.

California State Capitol. Department of General Services, Office of Architecture and Construction. Sacramento, 1964.

California's State Capitol. Compiled by Workers of the Writer's Program of Works Projects Administration in Northern California. California State Department of Education. Sacramento State Printing Office, 1942.

California State Library. California Room. *Capitol Black Book.* (Scrapbook of clippings and typed notes). Sacramento, California.

Caughey, John W. *History of California.* New York: Prentice Hall, 1940.

Clark, George. *Leland Stanford.* Stanford: Stanford University Press, 1931.

Cleland, Robert Glass. *The American Period.* New York: Macmillan, 1922.

Coy, Owen Cochran. *Pictorial History of California.* Davis: University Extension, 1926.

Crosby, Elisha Oscar. *Memoirs of Elisha Oscar Crosby.* San Marino: Huntington Library, 1945.

Delmatier, Royce, Clarence McIntosh, and Earl G. Waters. *Rumble of California Politics.* New York: John Wiley, 1970.

Dillon, Richard. *Fool's Gold.* New York: Coward McCann, Inc., 1967.

Dillon, Richard. *Great Expectations,* the Story of Benicia, California. Benicia Heritage Book, 1980.

Eldredge, Zoeth Skinner. *History of California.* Vol. III. New York: Century History Company, 1859.

Elliott, Janet. "History of the Seat of Government." Master's thesis, University of Pacific at Stockton, 1942.

Field, Stephen. *Personal Reminiscences of the Early Days of California.* Da Capo Press, 1968.

Foote, H. S. *Pen Pics from the Garden of the World or Santa Clara County, California.* Chicago: Lewis Publishing Co., 1888.

Girvigian, Raymond, F. A. I. A. and Associates. *Restoration and Development of the Capitol for the Joint Committee on Rules California State Legislature.* Vol. II. 1975, (unpublished).

Gregory, Thomas Jefferson. *History of Solano and Napa Counties.* Historic Record, 1912.

Gudde, Edwin W. *Bigler's Chronicles of the West.* Berkeley: University of California Press, 1962.

Hall, Fredric. *The History of San Jose and Surroundings.* San Francisco: Bancroft, 1871.

Hansen, Woodrow James. *The Search for Authority in California.* Oakland, Biobooks, 1960.

Hart, James D. *A Companion to California.* New York: Oxford University, 1978.

Historical Atlas. *Map of Santa Clara County.* San Francisco, Thompson and West, 1976.

History of Santa Clara County, California. San Francisco: Alley Bowen and Company, 1881.

Heisch, Edward Joseph. *California's Capitol Park at Sacramento.* Sacramento: Anderson Co., 1936.

Hittell, Theodore. *History of California.* Vol. III, IV. San Francisco: Pacific Press Pub. Co., 1885.

Hunt, Rockwell, *California's Stately Hall of Fame.* Stockton: College of Pacific, 1950.

Hunt, Rockwell, and Nellie van de Grift Sanchez. *A Short History of California.* New York, Crowell, 1929.

Hoover, Mildred Brooke, Hero Eugene Rensch and Ethel Grace Rensch. *Historic Spots in California.* Third edition. Revised by William N. Abeloe. Stanford: Stanford University Press, 1966.

Hutchinson, W. H. *California.* Palo Alto, Star Publishing Co., 1980.

James, William and George McMurry. *History of San Jose.* San Jose, Smith Printing Co., 1933.

Jarvis, Chester Edward. "The Capitals of California, 1849-1854." Master's thesis, University of California, Berkeley, 1942.

Johnson, Paul C. *Pictorial History of California.* Crown, 1972.

Jones, Herbert C. "The First Legislature of California." Address by Senator Herbert C. Jones before the California Historical Society, San Jose, December 10, 1949. Sacramento, Senate of California, 1950.

Kelly, William. *A Stroll through the Diggings of California.* Oakland: Biobooks, 1950.

Kirker, Harold. *California's Architectural Frontier.* San Marino: Huntington Library, 1960.

Knowland, Joseph R. *California: A Landmark History.* Oakland Tribune Press, 1941.

Loftis, Anne. *Where the Twain Did Meet.* New York: Macmillan, 1973.

Lynch, Jeremiah. *A Senator of the Fifties.* San Francisco: A. M. Robertson, 1911.

McKinstry, Hon. Elisha Williams. Oration of Elisha Williams McKinstry on the 21st. Anniversary of the Society of California Pioneers. San Francisco: 1871.

McKittrick, Myrtle. *Vallejo: Son of California.* Portland: Binsford and Mort, 1944.

Margo, Elizabeth. *Taming the Forty-niner.* New York: Rinehart Co., 1955.

Massey, Ernest de. *A Frenchman in the Gold Mines.* San Francisco: California Historical Society, 1927.

Melendy, H. Brett, and Benjamin J. Gilbert. *Governors of California.* Georgetown: Talisman Press, 1965.

Murphey, Marion Fisher. *Seven Stars for California.* Sonoma: Sonoma Printing, 1979.

Older, Cora. *When California Was Young.* (Photocopy of articles appearing in the *San Jose News,* 1916-17, 1926-27. (Available at San Jose Public Library).

Pitt, Leonard. *The Decline of the Californios.* Berkeley: University of California Press, 1966.

Rolle, Andrew. *California.* New York: Crowell, 1962.

Royce, Josiah. *California.* New York: Knopf, 1948.

Sawyer, Eugene. *History of Santa Clara County with Biographical Sketches.* Los Angeles: Historic Record, 1922.

Schuck, Oscar. *Representative and Leading Men of the Pacific.* San Francisco: Bacon and Co., 1870.

Severnson, Thor. *Sacramento: An Illustrated History, 1839-1874.* California Historical Society, 1973.

Sherman, William T. *Memoirs of General William T. Sherman.* Bloomington: Indiana University Press, 1957.

Smith, Jesse N. (ed.) *Sketches of Old Sacramento.* Sacramento: Sacramento County Historical Society, 1976.

Soulé, Frank, John Gibon and James Nisbet. *The Annals of San Francisco.* New York: G. P. Putnam, 1884.

Standiford, Edward. *Patterns of California History.* San Francisco: Canfield Press, 1975.

Taylor, Bayard. *El Dorado, or Adventures in the Path of Empire.* New York: G. N. Putnam, 1884.

Tinkham, George H. *California Men and Events.* Stockton: California Record Co., 1915.

Underhill, Reuben. *From Cowhides to Golden Fleece.* Stanford: Stanford University Press, 1939.

Watkins, T. H. *California, an Illustrated History.* Palo Alto: American West, 1972.

Willams, David A. *David C. Broderick, a Political Portrait.* San Marino: Huntington Library, 1969.

Winther, Oscar. *Story of San Jose, 1777-1869.* California Historical Society, 1935.

Wold, Gladys B. *Benicia History and Tour Guide.* Benicia Chamber of Commerce, 1971.

Woodward, Lucinda. *A Documentary History of California's State Capitol.* Sacramento: California State Restoration Project, 1981. (unpublished).

PERIODICALS

California Highway Patrolman

Davis, Elmer George. "How California Was Capitalized," (January, 1982), 44.

California Historical Society Quarterly

Barker, Charles. "E. O. Crosby, a California Lawyer," XXVII (1948), 133-40.

Bowman, J. N. "Cornerstone of the State Capitol: Its Discovery on October 15, 1952." XXXIII (1954), 329-335.

Bryant, Berryman. "Reminiscences of California, 1849-1852," XI (1932), 35-39.

Hussey, John. "The Old State House at Benicia: a Relic of California's Capital on Wheels," XVII (1938), 260-270.

Pomeroy, Earl. "California, 1846-1860, Politics of a Representative Frontier State," XXXII (1953), 291-302.

Radcliffe, Zoe Green. "Robert Baylor Semple," VI (1927), 130-158.

Watson, Douglas S. "An Hour's Walk Through Yerba Buena," XVII (1921), 291-302.

Wiltsee, Ernest, "The City of New York of the Pacific," XII (1921), 3-36.

Wright, Doris M. "The Making of Cosmopolitan California," XIX (1940), 338-42.

California Journal

Carroll, James R. "The Reconstructed Capitol: Safe, Elegant, Expensive. (January, 1982), 16.

Johnson, Charles. "Columbus: Notes and Comments," (January, 1973), 2.

Keppel, Bruce. "California's Pre-Fab Capitol," (December, 1975), 2.

"The Untold Story of the Greening of the Capitol," (July, 1973), 248.

Designers West

"Environment with a Mission: California State Capitol, a Historic and Working Museum," (May, 1982) 90.

Overland Monthly

Fields, M. H. "Grandma Bascom's Story of San Jose in '49," IX (1887), 543-551.

Rousseau, B. G. "Early History of the City of Vallejo," (August, 1923), 20-21.

Pacific Historical Review

Fredman, L. L. "Broderick, a Reassessment," XXX (1961), 39-46.

Melendy, Brett. "Who was John McDougal?" XXI (1960), 231-243.

Progressive Architecture

"To California with Love," (reprint from November, 1979), 5p.

Quarterly of the Society of California Pioneers

Cowan, Robert Ernest. "The Pioneers of California," VI (1929).

Van Sicklen, Helen Putnam. "The Life and Times of General M. G. Vallejo," IX (1932), 143-160.

Sacramento Magazine

Goodman, Jane. "A Stroll in the Park," (October, 1980).

NEWSPAPERS

Alta California

Dates as referred to in the text.

Sacramento Bee

The Sacramento Bee has chronicled events relating to the Capitol over the years. An index to pertinent material is available at the California State Library, California Room, Sacramento, California.

Special editions on the restoration:
"Restoring the Capitol." November 17, 1979
"The Restored Capitol." January 3, 1982.

Additionally, I recorded a number of interviews and talked with others informally.

Index

Brackets [   ] around page numbers indicate a picture.

LaVergne, TN USA
02 February 2010
171631LV00005B/3/P